William Shakespeare's
A MIDSUMMER NIGHT'S DREAM

Bloom's
NOTES

A CONTEMPORARY
LITERARY VIEWS BOOK

Edited and with an Introduction by
HAROLD BLOOM

3 5 7 9 8 6 4 2

Cover Illustration: Photofest

Library of Congress Cataloging-in-Publication Data

William Shakespeare's A midsummer night's dream / edited and with an introduction by Harold Bloom.
p. cm. – (Bloom's notes)
"Books by William Shakespeare":
Includes bibliographical references and index.
Summary: Includes a brief biography of the author, thematic and structural analysis of the work, critical views, and an index of themes and ideas.
ISBN 0-7910-4066-6
1. Shakespeare, William, 1564–1616. Midsummer night's dream. [1. Shakespeare, William, 1564–1616. Midsummer night's dream. 2. English literature—History and criticism.] I. Bloom, Harold. II. Series.
PR2827.B64 1995
822.3'3—dc20
95-43501
CIP
AC

Chelsea House Publishers
1974 Sproul Road, Suite 400
P.O. Box 914
Broomall, PA 19008-0914

Contents

User's Guide

This volume is designed to present biographical, critical, and bibliographical information on William Shakespeare and *A Midsummer Night's Dream.* Following Harold Bloom's introduction, there appears a detailed biography of the author, discussing the major events in his life and his important literary works. Then follows a thematic and structural analysis of the work, in which significant themes, patterns, and motifs are traced. An annotated list of characters supplies brief information on the chief characters in the work.

A selection of critical extracts, derived from previously published material by leading critics, then follows. The extracts consist of such things as statements by the author on his work, early notices of the work, and later evaluations down to the present day. The items are arranged chronologically by date of first publication. A bibliography of Shakespeare's writings (including a complete listing of all books he wrote, cowrote, edited, and translated, and selected posthumous publications), a list of additional books and articles on him and on *A Midsummer Night's Dream,* and an index of themes and ideas conclude the volume.

Harold Bloom is Sterling Professor of the Humanities at Yale University and Henry W. and Albert A. Berg Professor of English at the New York University Graduate School. He is the author of twenty books and the editor of more than thirty anthologies of literature and literary criticism.

Professor Bloom's works include *Shelley's Mythmaking* (1959), *The Visionary Company* (1961), *Blake's Apocalypse* (1963), *Yeats* (1970), *A Map of Misreading* (1975), *Kabbalah and Criticism* (1975), and *Agon: Towards a Theory of Revisionism* (1982). *The Anxiety of Influence* (1973) sets forth Professor Bloom's provocative theory of the literary relationships between the great writers and their predecessors. His most recent books are *The American Religion* (1992) and *The Western Canon* (1994).

Professor Bloom earned his Ph.D. from Yale University in 1955 and has served on the Yale faculty since then. He is a 1985 MacArthur Foundation Award recipient and served as the Charles Eliot Norton Professor of Poetry at Harvard University in 1987–88. He is currently the editor of the Chelsea House series Major Literary Characters and Modern Critical Views, and other Chelsea House series in literary criticism.

Introduction

HAROLD BLOOM

The complexities of *A Midsummer Night's Dream* are extraordinary, since the play involves four different levels of representation, which intermingle but never can wholly fuse. Theseus, duke of Athens, and his betrothed, the Amazon queen Hippolyta, belong to ancient mythology. The young, confused lovers—Hermia, Helena, Lysander, Demetrius—belong to all times, all places, as all young lovers necessarily have a common element. The fairies—Oberon, Titania, Puck—are in the world of folklore, or of magic. Finally, the "mechanicals" or artisans—Peter Quince, Flute, Snout, Snug, Starveling, and the sublime Bottom—come out of Shakespeare's countryside, and so are English rustics. Highly aware of the diversity of this melange, Shakespeare defines and defends his play in the wonderful exchanges between Theseus and Hippolyta concerning the music of the hounds in Act IV, scene 1, lines 103–127. Theseus commends "the musical confusion / of hounds and echo in conjunction," while Hippolyta recalls the hounds of Sparta: "I never heard / So musical a discord, such sweet thunder." Subtly, Shakespeare indicates the particular art of *A Midsummer Night's Dream:* to give us a musical confusion and discord of mythic beings, young lovers, fairies, and English rustics that together will produce "such sweet thunder."

A Midsummer Night's Dream might fly apart if it were not held together at its core by Bottom the weaver. A "bottom" means the center of the skein upon which a weaver's wool is wound, and it also means, more commonly, what we hear in a grand sentence from Montaigne's greatest essay, "Of Experience," which Shakespeare probably read from manuscript in John Florio's translation: "On the loftiest of the world's thrones we still are sitting on our own Bottom." Bottom, above all else, reminds us that Shakespeare should be credited with the invention of the human, as we particularly understand what it is to be human. Bottom has been called inept, hubristic, silly, excessively self-assertive, and (wrongly) not very bright, but none of this matters, since he is also charming, amiable, mild, good-natured, sweetly witty, courageous, kind, and even wise (though he denies this). Most vitally, Bottom is the one link between mortal men and women and the fairies in the play. Puck's victim, he transcends Puck and establishes his true relationship to the fairy world, not with the magically intoxicated Titania but with the more amiable foursome of Peaseblossom, Cobweb, Moth, and Mustardseed, all of them as gentle and innocent as himself.

Northrop Frye usefully points out that Bottom is the only mortal in the play who actually is capable of *seeing* the fairies. One can go further and say that Bottom is capable of seeing what St. Paul says cannot be seen:

> Eye hath not seen, nor ear heard, neither have entered into the heart of man, the things which God hath prepared for them that love him. But God hath revealed them unto us by his Spirit. (1 Corinthians 2:9–10)

Waking up from his bottomless dream, the weaver Bottom, who manifests natural, original goodness and not original sin, scrambles the language of this and fuses flesh and spirit in a synesthesia that Romantic poetry later will develop:

> The eye of man hath not heard, the ear of man hath not seen, man's hand is not able to taste, his tongue to conceive, nor his heart to report, what my dream was.

It is only a step from this to the visions of William Blake or of Wordsworth or Shelley. With Bottom, Shakespeare's invention of the human truly had begun, an invention we still live in, and by. ❖

Biography of William Shakespeare

Few events in the life of William Shakespeare are supported by reliable evidence, and many incidents recorded by commentators of the last four centuries are either conjectural or apocryphal.

William Shakespeare was born in Stratford-upon-Avon on April 22 or 23, 1564, the son of Mary Arden and John Shakespeare, a tradesman. His very early education was in the hands of a tutor, for his parents were probably illiterate. At age seven he entered the Free School in Stratford, where he learned the "small Latin and less Greek" attributed to him by Ben Jonson. When not in school Shakespeare may have gone to the popular Stratford fairs and to the dramas and mystery plays performed by traveling actors.

When Shakespeare was about thirteen his father removed him from school and apprenticed him to a butcher, although it is not known how long he remained in this occupation. When he was eighteen he married Anne Hathaway; their first child, Susanna, was born six months later. A pair of twins, Hamnet and Judith, were born in February 1585. About this time Shakespeare was caught poaching deer on the estate of Sir Thomas Lucy of Charlecot; Lucy's prosecution is said to have inspired Shakespeare to write his earliest literary work, a satire on his opponent. Shakespeare was convicted of poaching and forced to leave Stratford. He withdrew to London, leaving his family behind. He soon attached himself to the stage, initially in a menial capacity (as tender of playgoers' horses, according to one tradition), then as prompter's attendant. When the poaching furor subsided, Shakespeare returned to Stratford to join one of the many bands of itinerant actors. In the next five years he gained what little theater training he received.

By 1592 Shakespeare was a recognized actor, and in that year he wrote and produced his first play, *Henry VI, Part One*. Its success impelled Shakespeare soon afterward to write the second and third parts of *Henry VI*. (Many early and modern critics believed that *Love's Labour's Lost* preceded these histories as Shakespeare's earliest play, but the majority of modern scholars discount this theory.) Shakespeare's popularity provoked the jealousy of Robert Greene, as recorded in his posthumous *Groats-worth of Wit* (1592).

In 1593 Shakespeare published *Venus and Adonis,* a long poem based upon Ovid (or perhaps upon Arthur Golding's translation of Ovid's *Metamorphoses*). It was dedicated to the young earl of Southampton—but perhaps without permission, a possible indication that Shakespeare was trying to gain the nobleman's patronage. However, the dedicatory address to Southampton in the poem *The Rape of Lucrece* (1594) reveals Shakespeare to have been on good terms with him. Many plays—such as *Titus Andronicus, The Comedy of Errors,* and *Romeo and Juliet*—were produced over the next several years, most performed by Shakespeare's troupe, the Lord Chamberlain's Company. In December 1594 Shakespeare acted in a comedy (of unknown authorship) before Queen Elizabeth; many other royal performances followed in the next decade.

In August 1596 Shakespeare's son Hamnet died. Early the next year Shakespeare bought a home, New Place, in the center of Stratford; he is said to have planted a mulberry tree in the backyard with his own hands. Shakespeare's relative prosperity is indicated by his purchasing more than a hundred acres of farmland in 1602, a cottage near his estate later that year, and half-interest in the tithes of some local villages in 1605.

In September 1598 Shakespeare began his friendship with the then unknown Ben Jonson by producing his play *Every Man in His Humour.* The next year the publisher William Jaggard affixed Shakespeare's name, without his permission, to a curious medley of poems under the title *The Passionate Pilgrim;* the majority of the poems were not by Shakespeare. Two of his sonnets, however, appeared in this collection, although the 154 sonnets, with their mysterious dedication to "Mr. W. H.," were not published as a group until 1609. Also in 1599 the Globe Theatre was built in Southwark (an area of London), and Shakespeare's company began acting there. Many of his greatest plays—*Troilus and Cressida, King Lear, Othello, Macbeth*—were performed in the Globe before its destruction by fire in 1613.

The death in 1603 of Queen Elizabeth, the last of the Tudors, and the accession of James I, from the Stuart dynasty of Scotland, created anxiety throughout England. Shakespeare's fortunes, however, were unaffected, as the new monarch extended the license of Shakespeare's company to perform at the Globe. James I saw a performance of *Othello* at the court in November 1604. In October 1605 Shakespeare's company performed before the Mayor and Corporation of Oxford.

The last five years of Shakespeare's life seem void of incident; he had retired from the stage by 1613. Among the few known incidents is Shakespeare's involvement in a heated and lengthy dispute about the enclosure of common-fields around Stratford. He died on April 23, 1616, and was buried in the Church of St. Mary's in Stratford. A monument was later erected to him in the Poets' Corner of Westminster Abbey.

Numerous corrupt quarto editions of Shakespeare's plays were published during his lifetime. These editions, based on either manuscripts, promptbooks, or sometimes merely actors' recollections of the plays, were meant to capitalize on Shakespeare's renown. Other plays, now deemed wholly or largely spurious—*Edward III, The Yorkshire Tragedy, The Two Noble Kinsmen,* and others—were also published under Shakespeare's name during and after his lifetime. Shakespeare's plays were collected in the First Folio of 1623 by John Heminge and Henry Condell. Nine years later the Second Folio was published, and in 1640 Shakespeare's poems were collected. The first standard collected edition was by Nicholas Rowe (1709), followed by the editions of Alexander Pope (1723–1725), Lewis Theobald (1733), Samuel Johnson (1765), Edmond Malone (1790), and many others.

Shakespeare's plays are now customarily divided into the following categories (probable dates of writing are given in brackets): comedies (*The Comedy of Errors* [1590], *The Taming of the Shrew* [1592], *The Two Gentlemen of Verona* [1592–93], *A Midsummer Night's Dream* [1595], *Love's Labour's Lost* [1595], *The Merchant of Venice* [1596–98], *As You Like It* [1597], *The Merry Wives of Windsor* [1597], *Much Ado About Nothing* [1598–99], *Twelfth Night* [1601], *All's Well That Ends Well* [1603–04], and *Measure for Measure* [1604]); histories

(*Henry VI, Part One* [1590–92], *Henry VI, Parts Two and Three* [1590–92], *Richard III* [1591], *King John* [1591–98], *Richard II* [1595], *Henry IV, Part One* [1597], *Henry IV, Part Two* [1597], *Henry V* [1599], and *Henry VIII* [1613]); tragedies (*Titus Andronicus* [1590], *Romeo and Juliet* [1595], *Julius Caesar* [1599], *Hamlet* [1599–1601], *Troilus and Cressida* [1602], *Othello* [1602–04], *King Lear* [1604–05], *Macbeth* [1606], *Timon of Athens* [1607], *Antony and Cleopatra* [1606–07], and *Coriolanus* [1608]); romances (*Pericles, Prince of Tyre* [1606–08], *Cymbeline* [1609–10], *The Winter's Tale* [1610–11], and *The Tempest* [1611]). However, Shakespeare willfully defied the canons of classical drama by mingling comedy, tragedy, and history, so that in some cases classification is debatable or arbitrary.

Shakespeare's reputation, while subject to many fluctuations, was firmly established by the eighteenth century. Samuel Johnson remarked, "Perhaps it would not be easy to find any authour, except Homer, who invented so much as Shakespeare, who so much advanced the studies which he cultivated, who effused so much novelty upon his age or country. The form, the characters, the language, and the shows of the English drama are his." Early in the nineteenth century Samuel Taylor Coleridge declared, "The Englishman who without reverence, a proud and affectionate reverence, can utter the name of William Shakespeare, stands disqualified for the office of critic. . . . Great as was the genius of Shakespeare, his judgment was at least equal to it."

A curious controversy developed in the middle of the nineteenth century in regard to the authorship of Shakespeare's plays, some contending that Sir Francis Bacon was the actual author of the plays, others (including Mark Twain) advancing the claims of the earl of Oxford. None of these attempts has succeeded in persuading the majority of scholars that Shakespeare himself is not the author of the plays attributed to him.

In recent years many landmark editions of Shakespeare, with increasingly accurate texts and astute critical commentary, have emerged. These include the *Arden Shakespeare* (1951f.–) the *Oxford Shakespeare* (1982–), and the *New Cambridge*

Shakespeare (1984–). Such critics as T. S. Eliot, G. Wilson Knight, Northrop Frye, W. H. Auden, and many others have continued to elucidate Shakespeare, his work, and his times, and he remains the most written-about author in the history of English literature. ❖

Thematic and Structural Analysis

In **Act I** of *A Midsummer Night's Dream,* Shakespeare introduces the main human characters of his comedy and his play's
central themes, one of which is best expressed by this act's
well-known line: "The course of true love never did run
smooth." In some ways Lysander's declaration becomes the
play's structural and thematic point of departure, as the comedy interlocks the misadventures of five pairs of lovers—six if
one counts Pyramus and Thisby, who appear in Act V's play
within the play—and uses their tribulations to explore its
theme of love's difficulties. Central to the play is the tension
between desire and social mores; repeatedly characters will be
required to quell their passion for the sake of law and propriety. Another important conflict is between love and reason,
with the heart almost always overruling the mind. The comedy
of the play results from the powerful, and often blinding,
effects that love has on the characters' thoughts and actions.

The play opens in Athens, ruled by Theseus, who will wed
Hippolyta, queen of the Amazons, in four days (**I.1**). At the
start of the play, Theseus voices his impatience for his marriage, immediately establishing the disjunction between desire
and social dicta. The introduction of Egeus and his daughter
Hermia reinforces this conflict, for the pair has come to Theseus
to resolve a dispute over Hermia's future husband. Although
Egeus has promised Hermia in marriage to Demetrius, Hermia
wants to marry Lysander, who, Egeus complains, "[w]ith cunning hast . . . filched my daughter's heart." Egeus asserts his
paternal right to determine Hermia's husband, and Theseus
supports this, saying, "Be advised, fair maid / To you your
father should be a god." Hermia quickly shows that she is not
cowed by her father's decision or Theseus' decree, wishing
instead that the men consider her feelings. The strength of her
spirit and willpower are clear as she says to Theseus, "I would
that my father looked with my eyes," to which the duke
replies, "Rather your eyes with his judgment look."
Shakespeare employs images of eyes and eyesight throughout

the play; making continual reference to different characters' vision—that they see things differently and that they are often not sure of what they see—he suggests, among other things, that love deprives a person of clear sight and clear thought.

Hermia inquires what her choices are if she refuses to marry Demetrius, and Theseus proposes two options: to die or to become a nun. Theseus, newly in love himself, gently tries to persuade her to reconsider and gives her until the morning of his marriage day to make her final decision. The two suitors, Demetrius and Lysander, also assert themselves in this scene: Demetrius urges Hermia to obey the law and her father's will, while Lysander scornfully suggests that, as Demetrius has Egeus' love, the two marry and leave Hermia and himself alone. Lysander also suggests that Demetrius has been inconstant as a lover; he has already "made love to Nedar's daughter, Helena / And won her soul." Theseus admits that he had heard about Demetrius' involvement with Helena but had forgotten about it.

After Demetrius, Theseus, Egeus, and Hippolyta depart, Lysander and Hermia are left alone and swear their devotion to each other. Hermia's defiance is reasserted as she laments to Lysander, "O cross! . . . O spite! . . . O hell! to choose love by another's eyes." In order to escape the fate that awaits Hermia, Lysander suggests that they flee Athens to the home of his widowed aunt, where, beyond the constraints of Athenian law, they can be married. They agree to meet the next night in the woods outside Athens, and as the play progresses, it becomes clear that the woods—a place of magic and possibility—serve as a foil to the rational order of the Athenian court. Helena, Hermia's close friend who is in love with Demetrius, now comes upon the two, and Lysander reveals their plan to her:

> To-morrow night, when Phoebe doth behold
> Her silver visage in the wat'ry glass,
> Decking with liquid pearl the bladed grass
> A time that lovers' flights doth still conceal
> Through Athens' gates have we devis'd to steal.

The moon, in this scene and throughout the play, is a silent but crucial character. On a literal level, the moon is necessary to

illuminate the characters' nocturnal activities and so is a beneficent force, rendering love possible. Yet the moon is also nega-
tive, as when Theseus tells Hermia that as a "barren sister" (a
nun), she will spend her life "[c]hanting hymns to the cold fruitless moon." The title of the play alludes to Midsummer Night—
traditionally a time of revelry, magic, and transition; the woodland setting, the presence of the fairy world, the cover of darkness, and the presence of the moon evoke the mystery and
enchantments of this time.

In the scene's final speech, Helena decides to tell Demetrius
of Hermia and Lysander's elopement in hopes of gaining his
confidence and love, although it means betraying her best
friend: "[A]nd for this intelligence / If I have thanks, it is a dear
expense. / But herein mean I to enrich my pain, / To have his
sight thither and back again."

Act I, scene 2 opens with an assembly of local craftsmen.
Bottom the weaver, Flute the bellows-mender, Snout the tinker,
Starveling the tailor, Quince the carpenter, and Snug the joiner
hope to present a play at the wedding of Theseus and
Hippolyta and to be financially rewarded for their efforts. What
the craftsmen lack in professional experience they make up for
in enthusiasm. Quince immediately takes charge of the group,
giving out parts and direction. Their choice of play, "The most
lamentable comedy and most cruel death of Pyramus and
Thisby," builds on the theme of star-crossed lovers who must
decide their fate. It also demonstrates how Shakespeare juxta-
poses divergent elements to create comedy. It is unusual that a
tragic love story would be performed at a nuptial celebration,
yet in their eagerness the men overlook this. The text of *A
Midsummer Night's Dream* itself also reflects Shakespeare's
use of opposition. Employing a device he uses in many of his
plays, he has the characters at the Athenian court speak in
verse and the craftsmen speak in prose, emphasizing the contrast between the "high" and "low" elements of the play's
comedy.

As they plan their performance, each of the men begins to
assert his personality: Bottom volunteers for every part; Snug
confesses he is "slow of study" and wants only to play the role
of the lion, for it requires nothing except that he roar. The

craftsmen's only acknowledgment of the impropriety of their dramatic selection comes when, remembering that they will be at court, they mention that the "lion" must not "fright the ladies out of their wits." In his eagerness to play the part, Bottom, who is eventually cast as Pyramus, promises to roar like a dove or a nightingale. Quince asks the group to meet in the woods the next night for a rehearsal. Their bumbling earnestness is expressed by Bottom's exhortation that there there the troupe can "rehearse most obscenely and courageously."

In **Act II, scene 1** Shakespeare introduces the fairy world, whose presence is central to the play's aura of enchantment and mystery. As the act opens, a fairy is speaking with Robin Goodfellow, better known as Puck, who is chief attendant to Oberon, king of the fairies. The fairy, a servant to the fairy queen, Titania, details her duties: "I must go seek some dewdrops here, / And hang a pearl in every cowslip's ear." Likewise, Puck reveals his purposes: "I am that merry wanderer of the night. / I jest to Oberon and make him smile." He also confesses to playing household tricks: "The wisest aunt, telling the saddest tale, / Sometimes for a three-foot stool mistaketh me; / Then slip I from her bum, down topples she. . . ."

Puck reveals that there has been a quarrel between Titania and Oberon, who shortly enter with their trains. While Titania and Oberon are ethereal, spiritual creatures with magical powers, they clearly possess some very human emotions and are not above jealousy or revenge; they now accuse one another of infidelity. Titania mentions she has seen Oberon "versing love / To amorous Phillida" and of having loved Hippolyta. Oberon counters that she should not reprimand him when he knows of her love for Theseus. Their conflict has led to neglect of the earth, instigating "[c]ontagious fogs," floods, poor harvests, and sickness. Titania tells Oberon, "And this same progeny of evils comes / From our debate, from our dissension, / We are their parents and original." Their lovers' quarrel reintroduces the theme of love's difficulties—the jealousy, dissension, and soon confusion that the human characters will suffer as well.

Oberon proposes ending their argument if Titania will give him "a little changeling boy / To be [his] henchman," but Titania refuses. The boy in question is the child of a devotee of

Titania's, who has died in childbirth, and Titania has vowed to raise the child herself. Turning to metaphor, she recalls how she and the child's mother sat talking as they watched traders' ships come in: "[W]e have laugh'd to see the sails conceiv'd / And grow big-bellied with the wanton wind / Which she, with pretty and with swimming gait / Following—her womb then rich with my young squire— / Would imitate. . . ." Titania's fidelity to her former companion is touching and will be mirrored by an exchange between Helena and Hermia that likewise recalls their girlhood friendship. Titania then proposes a truce, which Oberon will not accept, because the queen still refuses to relinquish the child. The two part in anger.

Oberon, furious, calls upon Puck to help devise his revenge. The fairy king describes how he once watched Cupid shoot an arrow that missed its intended target—a young virgin's heart—and instead hit a white flower, which it turned purple "with love's wound." The juice of the flower, which is now called "love-in-idleness," is a powerful potion that, when squeezed on the eyelids of a sleeping person, will make the sleeper fall in love with the first creature he or she sees upon awakening. Oberon orders Puck to find the flower, and Puck, resolving to "put a girdle round the earth" in his rapid quest for it, departs.

Hearing others approach, Oberon renders himself invisible and watches an exchange between Demetrius and Helena, who has chased Demetrius through the woods as he searches for Lysander and Hermia. Demetrius, intending to kill Lysander and win Hermia, is hardhearted toward Helena, who declares that despite his harsh words she still loves him: "Use me but as your spaniel, spurn me, strike me, / Neglect me, lose me; only give me leave / Unworthy as I am, to follow you." Demetrius claims that he becomes sick when he looks at her, while Helena becomes sick when she does not look at him—again, Shakespeare's joining of opposites. Demetrius threatens to run from Helena and leave her to the wild beasts. She implores him to reconsider, scolding him for his cruelty: "Fie, Demetrius! / Your wrongs do set a scandal on my sex. / We cannot fight for love as men may do; / We should be woo'd, and were not made to woo." Demetrius at last leaves, and Helena vows again to follow him. Thus, although Helena is initially characterized as more docile than Hermia, she shows herself to be quite as determined.

Puck returns with the magic flower, and Oberon instructs him to anoint Titania's sleeping eyes with it. Having observed the scene between Demetrius and Helena, Oberon also tells Puck to anoint the eyes of a "disdainful youth," whom Puck will recognize "by the Athenian garments he hath on." He seeks to reverse the situation so that Demetrius will pursue Helena and "prove / More fond on her than she upon her love."

Act II, scene 2 opens with Titania being sung to sleep by her fairies, who wish her safe rest and chant spells to ward off evil spirits. Upon finishing, they leave to attend to their duties: "Some to kill cankers in the musk-rose buds / Some to war with reremice [bats] for their leathern wings. . . ." In spite of their protective charms, as soon as Titania is asleep, Oberon steals in and squeezes the love potion on her eyelids, chanting,

> What thou seest when thou dost wake,
> Do it for thy true-love take. . . .
> Be it ounce [lynx] or cat, or bear,
> Pard [panther], or boar with bristled hair,
> In thy eye that shall appear
> When thou wak'st, it is thy dear.
> Wake when some vile thing is near.

Hermia and Lysander next enter, having lost their way in the woods. They agree to rest and begin a playful argument over how near to each other they should sleep. Because they are to be married, Lysander declares, "One turf shall serve as pillow for us both, / One heart, one bed, two bosoms, and one troth." Yet Hermia protests, "Lie further off, in human modesty. / Such separation as may well be said / Becomes a virtuous bachelor and a maid." Hermia wishes Lysander good night, saying, "With half that wish the wisher's eyes be press'd," words that with Puck's entrance take on further significance.

Puck espies the two asleep, and, seeing that they are not lying side by side and observing Lysander's Athenian garb, he takes Lysander for the youth about whom Oberon spoke. He anoints his eyes: "Churl, upon thy eyes I throw / All the power this charm doth owe. . . ."

After Puck departs, Demetrius enters with Helena still in hot pursuit. As she pauses to catch her breath, Demetrius runs off. In yet another allusion to eyes and eyesight, Helena speaks enviously of how attractive Hermia is while, she, Helena, feels so unwanted and forlorn: "Happy is Hermia, wheresoe'er she lies, / For she hath blessed and attractive eyes." Helena does not know that Hermia is nearby or that their situations will be reversed shortly. She soon sees Lysander and, not knowing if he is asleep or dead, wakes him. Lysander starts up and, true to the love potion's power, falls instantly in love with Helena.

Lysander repudiates his former love, swearing it is "not Hermia, but Helena I love: / Who will not change a raven for a dove?" The very sight of Hermia "[t]he deepest loathing to the stomach brings." Lysander's language becomes florid as he ironically attributes his change of affections to clear thinking: "And touching now the point of human skill, / Reason becomes marshall to my will, / And leads me to your eyes, where I o'er-look / Love's stories, written in Love's richest book." Helena, bewildered by his behavior and certain that she is being mocked, chastises Lysander and laments, "O, that a lady, of one man refus'd, / Should of another therefore be abus'd!" The two exit, and Hermia awakes, upset by a prophetic nightmare that a serpent was crawling on her breast and eating at her heart while Lysander "sat smiling at his cruel prey." She is terrified by Lysander's absence and leaves in search of him.

Act III begins with another installment of the night's activities in the woods, as the craftsmen assemble to rehearse their play (**III.1**). They discuss details of the plot—whether Pyramus should draw a sword to kill himself and whether this will upset the ladies of the court. In an even more absurd twist, Bottom suggests that the play's prologue should explain that the actors are not really being killed and that Pyramus is actually Bottom the weaver. Snout proposes also mentioning that the lion is really an actor and advises that the actor's face remain visible to assure the ladies doubly of their safety. Working out other details of the production, they consult the almanac to find out if there is to be moonlight on the night of their performance.

As they begin to rehearse, Puck enters unseen and starts to make trouble. Spooked, the actors all flee except for Bottom, upon whom Puck places an ass's head. Snout reenters and cries, "O Bottom, thou art chang'd." Bottom, unaware of his transformation, believes he is being mocked, and there is much subsequent punning on the phrase "To make an ass of me."

Puck then leads Bottom to Titania, who wakes and falls instantly in love with him. In response to her declaration of love, the confused Bottom speaks a line that captures one of the play's key themes: "[T]o say the truth, reason and love keep little company together nowadays." For this sagacity, Titania tells Bottom, "Thou art as wise as thou art beautiful." She wills him to stay and summons four fairies—Peaseblossom, Cobweb, Moth, and Mustardseed—to serve Bottom, who greatly enjoys his changed status without understanding its source. There is a lighthearted exchange between the fairies and Bottom, in which we gain greater insight into the fairy world and its activities.

Puck reports this turn of events to Oberon, who is delighted (**III.2**). Puck also tells his king that he has "latched" the eyes of the Athenian youth. Demetrius and Hermia soon come into view, Hermia frantic with concern for Lysander's well-being and fearful that Demetrius has done him harm. She scolds Demetrius ("Out, dog! Out, cur!") and says she has lost patience with his wooing. When Hermia leaves, angry and disgusted, Demetrius decides to rest and lies down to sleep. Oberon quickly realizes Puck's mistake: There is "[s]ome true-love turned, and not a false turned true." Oberon, upset by this error, commands Puck to fly through the woods until he finds Helena and to lead her to the sleeping Demetrius, whose eyes Oberon will "charm . . . against she do appear."

Oberon then anoints Demetrius' eyes and chants a charm. Puck returns with Helena and Lysander and, anticipating the coming events, speaks another of the play's most-famed lines: "Lord, what fools these mortals be!"

Lysander is pleading with Helena, who still believes that he is mocking her. Demetrius then wakes and sees Helena, with whom he falls instantly in love. His speech becomes overblown: "O Helen, goddess, nymph, perfect, divine!" In a neat reversal of the plot, where before both men loved

Hermia, they now both love Helena, who also takes on the vibrancy and vigor previously ascribed to Hermia. Helena exclaims, "O spite! Oh hell! I see you all are bent / To set against me for your merriment. . . . If you were men, as men you are in show, / You would not use a gentle lady so. . . ." Lysander and Demetrius have begun to quarrel over who loves Helena more when Hermia enters the scene. After Lysander refuses her affections, she is as bewildered as Helena. Helena, however, thinks that Hermia is involved in a conspiracy to mock her and believes herself further betrayed. In a touching speech, Helena appeals to Hermia, reminding her of their childhood friendship: "So we grew togeth'r / Like to a double cherry, seemingly parted, / But yet an union in partition, / Two lovely berries moulded on one stem; / So, with two seeming bodies, but one heart. . . ." This speech, reminiscent of Lysander's earlier words to Hermia ("[o]ne heart, one bed, two bosoms, and one troth"), reflects Shakespeare's theme of twinning: The two girls were once like twins, and their situation now makes them mirror opposites.

Hermia is amazed and insulted by Helena's accusation that she, as a joke, is making Lysander woo Helena and having Demetrius pretend to love her again. The two men continue meanwhile to vie for Helena's affection and begin to speak more harshly to Hermia, now mocking her dark complexion and short stature. Anger grows between the two women. Helena appeals again to Hermia, saying she was always a loyal friend and only revealed the elopement to Demetrius so that she could follow him. Shakespeare sets up more comedy through the pairing of opposites; as Hermia is mocked for her short stature—" 'Little' again? nothing but 'low' and 'little'?" she cries in amazement—she in turn calls Helena a "painted maypole."

Lysander and Demetrius leave, presumably to duel over Helena's affection, and Hermia and Helena, now both enraged, are left alone. Oberon and Puck, who have witnessed the scene, seek a way to set things right. Oberon tells Puck to lead the men astray and to shroud the forest in fog so they cannot fight. When Lysander lies down to sleep, Puck is to anoint his eyes with the antidote to love-in-idleness, "[w]hose liquor hath this virtuous property, / To take from thence all error with his might / And make his eyeballs roll with wonted sight." Oberon will also ask Titania for the child, and, when she acquiesces, he will release "her charmed eye . . . from monster's view," remarking that then "all things shall be peace."

Puck, making haste because "Aurora's harbinger," the dawn, is approaching, departs to lead Lysander and Demetrius through the woods. He keeps them from one another's sight by mimicking in turn the voice and movements of each man in yet a further instance of doubling. Exhausted by their chase, the men finally lie down to sleep, and Puck applies the antidote to Lysander's eyes. Helena, weary with wandering and distress, lies down, hoping that sleep, "that sometimes shuts up sorrow's eye," will "[s]teal [her] awhile from [her] own company." Hermia, equally spent and miserable, soon lies down, remarking, "[M]y legs can keep no pace with my desires." Puck admits, "Cupid is a knavish lad, / Thus to make poor females mad."

Act IV, scene 1 finds Titania lovingly placing roses in Bottom's mane and her fairies still doting on his every whim. When she falls asleep with Bottom cradled in her arms, Oberon and Puck enter. Oberon begins to feel some remorse for his actions and tells Puck that Titania has yielded to his demand and sent him the child. Having gotten what he wanted, Oberon releases Titania from the spell. She awakens, bewildered: "My Oberon, what visions have I seen! / Methought I was enamored of an ass." After Titania recoils at the sight of Bottom, Oberon tells Puck to remove the ass's head from the weaver. The king and queen appear reconciled, and Oberon says, "Come, my queen, take hands with me. . . . Now thou and I are new in amity. . . ." The pair exit with the amazed Titania asking, "Tell me how it came this night / That I sleeping here was found / With these mortals on the ground."

After the fairies leave, Theseus enters with his train, which includes Hippolyta and Egeus. They are on a hunting party but soon come upon the four Athenians mysteriously sleeping in the wood. Theseus recognizes Hermia and remembers that it is her day to respond to his edict. The four waken and become confused when asked how they came to be in the woods. Lysander replies, "Half sleep, half waking; but as yet, I swear, /

I cannot truly say how I came here." He confesses that he and Hermia were planning to elope, angering Egeus. Demetrius can remember that Helena revealed the plan and that he intended to follow the lovers but now claims to love only Helena: "To her, my lord / Was I betrothed ere I saw Hermia / But, as in health, come to my natural taste, / Now I do wish it, love it, long for it. / And will for evermore be true to it."

Upon hearing about Demetrius' change of heart, Theseus makes a decision: "Egeus, I will overbear your will; / For in the temple, by and by, with us / These couples shall eternally be knit." The hunting trip is suspended, and the group departs for Athens, resolved to hear the tales of the night, though the four lovers agree that they are unsure of the events. "Methinks I see these things with parted eye / When everything seems double," says Hermia. And Demetrius wonders, "Are you sure / That we are awake? It seems to me / That yet we sleep, we dream."

The group departs, and the last of the night's dreamers awakens. Bottom, who is now alone in the woods, thinks that he is still in rehearsal and speaks of having a strange dream. "Man is but an ass if he go about to expound this dream," he comments, again expressing the idea of accepting misunderstanding and uncertainty: "The eye of man hath not heard, the ear of man hath not seen, man's hand is not able to taste, his tongue to conceive, nor his heart to report, what my dream was." The mixing up of body parts and their functions both literally and figuratively reflects the night's confusions, inversions of relationships, and blurrings of dream and reality. He speaks of getting Quince to write a ballet humorously called " 'Bottom's Dream', because it has no bottom."

The act ends with the rest of the craftsmen frantically preparing their play (**IV.2**). They are alarmed that there has been no sign of Bottom and wonder how their play might go on without him, for Bottom "hath simply the best wit of any handicraft man in Athens." Snug reports that the duke is approaching the temple with "two or three lords and ladies more married," while Flute complains that Bottom has cost them their financial reward. Bottom suddenly appears on the scene, instantly takes charge, and says that he will recount his adventures later, promising, in a further pun on his name, "I will tell you everything, right as it fell out."

The single scene of **Act V** begins with Hippolyta and Theseus speaking about the oddness of the lovers' tales of the night. "The lunatic, the lover, and the poet / Are of imagination all compact," says Theseus. Each is unique in his perception of reality, with the poet so steeped in his imagination that he can almost create his own world from his fantasies:

> The poet's eye, in a fine frenzy rolling,
> Doth glance from heaven to earth, from earth to heaven;
> And as imagination bodies forth
> The forms of things unknown, the poet's pen
> Turns them to shapes, and gives to airy nothing
> A local habitation and a name.
> Such tricks hath such strong imagination
> That, if it would but apprehend some joy,
> It comprehends some bringer of joy;
> Or in the night, imagining some fear,
> How easy is a bush suppos'd a bear?

The lovers enter, and they speak of the entertainments that will occupy them until they can retire to bed and consummate their marriages. Theseus asks Philostrate, his master of revels, what "abridgment" he has for the evening, and Philostrate presents a list of possible plays. Theseus is intrigued by the mention of " '[a] tedious brief scene of young Pyramus / And his love Thisby; very tragical mirth' " and, upon hearing that it is presented by Athenian craftsmen, orders it performed. He respects the actors' earnestness, saying, "For never anything can be amiss / When simpleness and duty tender it." Although Hippolyta protests that she does not like poor theater, Theseus insists that they view the production.

The play begins with Quince giving the prologue. In his nervous desire to please, however, he declares, "If we offend, it is with our good will," saying the opposite of what he intends and leading Theseus to comment that "[h]is speech was like a tangled chain; nothing impaired, but all disordered." In an interesting reversal, the craftsmen now speak in verse and the members of the court in prose. The prologue continues by giving a synopsis of the tragic fate of Pyramus and Thisby.

Separated by a wall through which they can only whisper, the lovers plan to meet secretly at Ninus' tomb. Thisby arrives first but is scared by a lion and flees, dropping her mantle, which the lion bloodies. Pyramus arrives, sees the bloody cloak, and, believing Thisby dead, stabs himself. Thisby, distraught, then stabs herself with Pyramus' dagger.

When Wall (Snout) presents his speech, Theseus asks, "Would you desire lime and hair to speak better?" Hippolyta, however, is not impressed, muttering, "This is the silliest stuff that ever I heard." Theseus replies, "The best in this kind are but shadows; and the worst are no worse, if imagination amend them." Snug, who plays the lion, includes a disclaimer that assures the ladies of his true identity as Snug the joiner. Theseus reflects, "A very gentle beast, and of a good conscience." The play continues with the appearance of Starveling as Moonshine and with Demetrius and Theseus commenting generally on the action as Hippolyta complains. Finally all catch the play's ridiculous spirit and begin to respond to the actors: Demetrius saying, "Well roared, Lion"; Theseus, "Well run, Thisby"; Hippolyta, "Well shone, Moon. Truly, the moon shines with a good grace"; and Theseus, "Well moused, Lion."

At the end of the play, Theseus reassures the actors that there is no need of an epilogue, "for [their] play needs no excuse." There is a dance instead, and finally Theseus proclaims, "The iron tongue of midnight hath told twelve. / Lovers, to bed; 'tis almost fairy time."

The lovers exit, and Puck, the spirit in charge of housekeeping, enters with a broom. He tells the audience that, during this enchanted time of night, "[n]ot a mouse / Shall disturb this hallowed house. / I am sent with broom before, / To sweep the dust behind the door." Oberon, Titania, and their trains enter, and Oberon tells his fairies, "And each several chambers bless, / Through this palace, with sweet peace; / And the owner of it blest / Ever shall in safety rest. / Trip away; make no stay; meet me all by break of day." Once again, the night is described as the domain of the fairy world, which interacts with and shapes the fate of the human world. Yet, in this closing scene, the benevolence of the world of spirits is established.

Puck ends the drama with a speech that further toys with the comedy's play between illusion and reality:

> If we shadows have offended,
> Think but this, and all is mended
> That you have but slumb'red here
> While these visions did appear
> And this weak and idle theme,
> No more yielding but a dream.

Calling himself "an honest Puck" who has meant no harm, he utters the play's closing lines, "So, good night unto you all. / Give me your hands, if we be friends, / And Robin shall restore amends." ❖

—*Elline Lipkin*

List of Characters

Theseus, duke of Athens, has the authority to determine the future of the play's human lovers. He is himself newly in love with Hippolyta, whose land he has won in a recent battle, and with whom he is engaged to be married. His wisdom is reflected in the respect that the other characters accord him.

Hippolyta, queen of the Amazons, has a relatively small role in the play. We learn that Theseus has conquered both her country and her heart. Her role reverses from one of (presumed) capability and authority to one of passivity, although her vehement criticism of the craftsmen's play suggests, ironically, a greater role than is ostensible. As Theseus' bride-to-be, she is half of one love relationship that has not suffered from confusion and mishap.

Hermia is a young Athenian woman who wishes to marry Lysander, although her father instead has arranged for her to marry Demetrius. Described as short, dark, spirited, and willful, Hermia expresses her choice of husband to Theseus, who decrees that she must obey her father's will, become a nun, or die. Again showing a fierce streak of determination, she agrees to Lysander's plan to elope, and when the two become lost in the woods, the play's "midsummer madness" begins.

Helena is Hermia's best friend and, serving as Hermia's mirror opposite, is described as tall and blond. In love with Demetrius, her suitor before his affections changed, Helena tries to win him back, going so far as to betray Hermia's plan to elope. Although generally characterized as less spirited than Hermia, she reveals her determination when she follows Demetrius through the woods as he searches for the lovers, and she holds her own during the confusion that ensues.

Lysander is Hermia's beloved and suggests that they elope. However, his affections change when Puck mistakenly applies love-juice to his eyes, and he falls in love with Helena. Ultimately, the antidote is applied, and he marries Hermia.

Demetrius is Lysander's dramatic double, as Helena is Hermia's. He is also in love with Hermia, who does not love him, and is her father's choice of suitor. He wooed Helena, however, before transferring his affections to Hermia, and so earned a reputation for inconstancy. When he follows the lovers into the woods, he comes under the love-juice's power and falls in love with Helena again, marrying her at the end of the play.

Egeus is Hermia's father. His command that she marry Demetrius instead of Lysander sets the play's action in motion, causing Hermia and Lysander, fleeing Athenian laws, to escape to the woods—the magical locale of the fairies.

Oberon, king of the fairies, has magical powers that affect the earth's seasons. Although a spirit, he possesses human traits such as jealousy and anger, which lead him to wreak his comic revenge on Titania. The love-juice he orders Puck to administer first to Titania and then to Lysander and Demetrius is responsible for much of the play's confusion.

Titania, queen of the fairies, is embroiled in a dispute with Oberon because she refuses to give him the orphaned human child of one of her devotees for his attendant. Her touching loyalty mirrors the sentiments of friendship that Helena voices in an exchange with Hermia. Titania becomes a victim of Oberon's revenge when Puck administers love-juice to her eyes and presents the newly transformed Nick Bottom, with whom she instantly falls in love. In spite of these goings-on, she and Oberon are reconciled at the end of the play.

Puck, or Robin Goodfellow, is Oberon's attendant and, acting on the king's commands, carries out most of the play's mischief. Known as a household spirit, Puck's first speech describes many of the tricks he plays on housewives. At the end of the play, he appears with a broom, ready to tidy the stage and restore order to the households of the newly married couples. He asks forgiveness for his trickery, reminding listeners that all he does is in good spirits.

Peaseblossom, Cobweb, Moth, and Mustardseed are Titania's fairy attendants, whom the queen orders to serve her new love, Bottom. The descriptions of their duties illuminate the activities of the fairy world.

Nick Bottom, a weaver, is among the craftsmen who decide to put on a play for Theseus' wedding. While rehearsing in the woods for his role as *Pyramus,* Bottom becomes the vehicle of Oberon's revenge on Titania when Puck transforms the weaver into a creature with an ass's head and leads him into the enchanted Titania's sight. Bottom enjoys his status as Titania's beloved without realizing his transformation. When he is changed back, he is unsure of what has happened to him, and his speech reiterates the larger theme that things are never quite what they seem.

Peter Quince/Prologue, Francis Flute/Thisby, Tom Snout/Wall, Snug/Lion, and Robin Starveling/Moonshine are the other members of the cast of the craftsmen's play. Speaking in prose (except for the absurd poetry of their play) and exhibiting a general lack of sophistication, the craftsmen stand in comic contrast to the play's other characters. ✤

Critical Views

[August Wilhelm von Schlegel (1767–1845) was a leading German critic who significantly influenced many English writers of the Romantic period. In his famous book, *Lectures on Dramatic Art and Literature* (1809–11), excerpted here, Schlegel praises *A Midsummer Night's Dream* as a triumph of fantastic imagination in its depiction of the fairy world.]

In *The Midsummer Night's Dream*, on the other hand, there flows a luxuriant vein of the boldest and most fantastical invention; the most extraordinary combination of the most dissimilar ingredients seems to have been brought about without effort by some ingenious and lucky accident, and the colours are of such clear transparency that we think the whole of the variegated fabric may be blown away with a breath. The fairy world here described resembles those elegant pieces of arabesque, where little genii with butterfly wings rise, half embodied, above the flower-cups. Twilight, moonshine, dew, and spring perfumes, are the element of these tender spirits; they assist nature in embroidering her carpet with green leaves, many-coloured flowers, and glittering insects; in the human world they do but make sport childishly and waywardly with their beneficent or noxious influences. Their most violent rage dissolves in good-natured raillery; their passions, stripped of all earthly matter, are merely an ideal dream. To correspond with this, the loves of mortals are painted as a poetical enchantment, which, by a contrary enchantment, may be immediately suspended, and then renewed again. The different parts of the plot; the wedding of Theseus and Hippolyta, Oberon and Titania's quarrel, the flight of the two pair of lovers, and the theatrical manœuvres of the mechanics, are so lightly and happily interwoven that they seem necessary to each other for the formation of a whole. Oberon is desirous of relieving the lovers from their perplexities, but greatly adds to them through the mistakes of his minister, till he at last comes really to the aid of their fruitless amorous pain, their inconstancy and jealousy, and restores fidelity to its old rights. The extremes of fanciful and vulgar are united when the enchanted Titania awakes and falls in love with a coarse mechanic with an ass's head, who represents, or rather disfigures, the part of a tragical lover. The droll wonder of Bottom's transformation is merely the translation of a metaphor in its literal sense; but in his behaviour during the tender homage of the Fairy Queen we have an amusing proof how much the consciousness of such a head-dress heightens the effect of his usual folly. Theseus and Hippolyta are, as it were, a splendid frame for the picture; they take no part in the action, but surround it with a stately pomp. The discourse of the hero and his Amazon, as they course through the forest with their noisy hunting-train, works upon the imagination like the fresh breath of morning, before which the shapes of night disappear. Pyramus and Thisbe is not unmeaningly chosen as the grotesque play within the play; it is exactly like the pathetic part of the piece, a secret meeting of two lovers in the forest, and their separation by an unfortunate accident, and closes the whole with the most amusing parody.

—August Wilhelm von Schlegel, *Lectures on Dramatic Art and Literature* (1809–11), tr. John Black (1816), rev. A. S. W. Morrison (London: George Bell & Sons, 1846), pp. 393–94

WILLIAM HAZLITT ON BOTTOM AND PUCK

[William Hazlitt (1778–1830) was one of the leading British essayists of the early nineteenth century. Among his many works are *Lectures on the English Poets* (1818), *Lectures on the English Comic Writers* (1819), *The Spirit of the Age* (1825), and a moving account of his love affair with a coquette, *Liber Amoris* (1823). In his important treatise, *Characters of Shakespear's Plays* (1817), Hazlitt studies the contrasting characters of Bottom and Puck.]

Bottom the Weaver is a character that has not had justice done him. He is the most romantic of mechanics. And what a list of

30

companions he has—Quince the Carpenter, Snug the Joiner, Flute the Bellows-mender, Snout the Tinker, Starveling the Tailor; and then again, what a group of fairy attendants, Puck, Peaseblossom, Cobweb, Moth, and Mustard-seed! It has been observed that Shakespear's characters are constructed upon deep physiological principles; and there is something in this play which looks very like it. Bottom the Weaver, who takes the lead of

> This crew of patches, rude mechanicals,
> That work for bread upon Athenian stalls,

follows a sedentary trade, and he is accordingly represented as conceited, serious, and fantastical. He is ready to undertake any thing and every thing, as if it was as much a matter of course as the motion of his loom and shuttle. He is for playing the tyrant, the lover, the lady, the lion. 'He will roar that it shall do any man's heart good to hear him'; and this being objected to as improper, he still has a resource in his good opinion of himself, and 'will roar you an 'twere any nightingale.' Snug the Joiner is the moral man of the piece, who proceeds by measurement and discretion in all things. You see him with his rule and compasses in his hand. 'Have you the lion's part written? Pray you, if it be, give it me, for I am slow of study.'—'You may do it extempore,' says Quince, 'for it is nothing but roaring.' Starveling the Tailor keeps the peace, and objects to the lion and the drawn sword. 'I believe we must leave the killing out when all's done.' Starveling, however, does not start the objections himself, but seconds them when made by others, as if he had not spirit to express his fears without encouragement. It is too much to suppose all this intentional: but it very luckily falls out so. Nature includes all that is implied in the most subtle analytical distinctions; and the same distinctions will be found in Shakespear. Bottom, who is not only chief actor, but stage-manager for the occasion, has a device to obviate the danger of frightening the ladies: 'Write me a prologue, and let the prologue seem to say, we will do no harm with our swords, and that Pyramus is not killed indeed; and for better assurance, tell them that I, Pyramus, am not Pyramus, but Bottom the Weaver: this will put them out of fear.' Bottom seems to have understood the subject of dramatic illusion at least as well as any modern essayist. If our holiday mechanic rules the roast among his fellows, he is no less at home in his new character of an ass, 'with amiable cheeks, and fair large ears.' He instinctively acquires a most learned taste, and grows fastidious in the choice of dried peas and bottled hay. He is quite familiar with his new attendants, and assigns them their parts with all due gravity. 'Monsieur Cobweb, good Monsieur, get your weapon in your hand, and kill me a red-hipt humble bee on the top of a thistle, and, good Monsieur, bring me the honey-bag.' What an exact knowledge is here shewn of natural history!

Puck, or Robin Goodfellow, is the leader of the fairy band. He is the Ariel of the *Midsummer Night's Dream;* and yet as unlike as can be to the Ariel in *The Tempest.* No other poet could have made two such different characters out of the same fanciful materials and situations. Ariel is a minister of retribution, who is touched with the sense of pity at the woes he inflicts. Puck is a mad-cap sprite, full of wantonness and mischief, who laughs at those whom he misleads—'Lord, what fools these mortals be!' Ariel cleaves the air, and executes his mission with the zeal of a winged messenger; Puck is borne along on his fairy errand like the light and glittering gossamer before the breeze. He is, indeed, a most Epicurean little gentleman, dealing in quaint devices, and faring in dainty delights. Prospero and his world of spirits are a set of moralists: but with Oberon and his fairies we are launched at once into the empire of the butterflies. How beautifully is this race of beings contrasted with the men and women actors in the scene, by a single epithet which Titania gives to the latter, 'the human mortals!' It is astonishing that Shakespear should be considered, not only by foreigners, but by many of our own critics, as a gloomy and heavy writer, who painted nothing but 'gorgons and hydras, and chimeras dire.' His subtlety exceeds that of all other dramatic writers, insomuch that a celebrated person of the present day said that he regarded him rather as a metaphysician than a poet. His delicacy and sportive gaiety are infinite. In the *Midsummer Night's Dream* alone, we should imagine, there is more sweetness and beauty of description than in the whole range of French poetry put together. What we mean is this, that we will produce out of that single play ten passages, to which we do not think any ten passages in the works of the French poets can be opposed, displaying equal fancy and imagery. Shall we mention the remonstrance of Helena to Hermia, or Titania's description of her fairy train, or her disputes with Oberon about the Indian boy, or Puck's account of himself and his employments, or the Fairy Queen's exhortation to the elves to pay due attendance upon her favourite, Bottom; or Hippolita's description of a chace, or Theseus's answer? The two last are as heroical and spirited as the others are full of luscious tenderness. The reading of this play is like wandering in a grove by moonlight: the descriptions breathe a sweetness like odours thrown from beds of flowers.

—William Hazlitt, *Characters of Shakespear's Plays* (1817), *The Complete Works of William Hazlitt*, ed. P. P. Howe (London: J. M. Dent & Sons, 1930), Vol. 4, pp. 244–46

G. K. Chesterton on the "Mysticism of Happiness" in *A Midsummer Night's Dream*

[G. K. Chesterton (1874–1926) is today perhaps best known for his Father Brown detective stories, but he was also a prolific essayist, critic, and philosopher. Among his works are monographs on Robert Browning (1903), Charles Dickens (1906), and George Bernard Shaw (1910). In this extract (taken from an essay in his book, *The Common Man* [1904]), Chesterton praises *A Midsummer Night's Dream* and argues that its sentiment can be summed up as "the mysticism of happiness."]

The greatest of Shakespeare's comedies is also, from a certain point of view, the greatest of his plays. No one would maintain that it occupied this position in the matter of psychological study if by psychological study we mean the study of individual characters in a play. No one would maintain that Puck was a character in the sense that Falstaff is a character, or that the critic stood awed before the psychology of Peaseblossom. But there is a sense in which the play is perhaps a greater triumph of psychology than *Hamlet* itself. It may well be questioned whether in any other literary work in the world is so vividly rendered a social and spiritual atmosphere. There is an atmosphere in *Hamlet,* for instance, a somewhat murky and even melodramatic one, but it is subordinate to the great character, and morally inferior to him; the darkness is only a background for the isolated star of intellect. But *A Midsummer Night's Dream* is a psychological study, not of a solitary man, but of a spirit that unites mankind. The six men may sit talking in an inn; they may not know each other's names or see each other's faces before or after, but night or wine or great stories, or some rich and branching discussion may make them all at one, if not absolutely with each other, at least with that invisible seventh man who is the harmony of all of them. That seventh man is the hero of *A Midsummer Night's Dream.*

A study of the play from a literary or philosophical point of view must therefore be founded upon some serious realization of what this atmosphere is. In a lecture upon *As You Like It,* Mr. Bernard Shaw made a suggestion which is an admirable example of his amazing ingenuity and of his one most interesting limitation. In maintaining that the light sentiment and optimism of the comedy were regarded by Shakespeare merely as the characteristics of a more or less cynical pot-boiler, he actually suggested that the title 'As You Like it' was a taunting address to the public in disparagement of their taste and the dramatist's own work. If Mr. Bernard Shaw had conceived of Shakespeare as insisting that Ben Jonson should wear Jaeger underclothing or join the Blue Ribbon Army, or distribute little pamphlets for the non-payment of rates, he could scarcely have conceived anything more violently opposed to the whole spirit of Elizabethan comedy than the spiteful and priggish modernism of such a taunt. Shakespeare might make the fastidious and cultivated Hamlet, moving in his own melancholy and purely mental world, warn players against an over-indulgence towards the rabble. But the very soul and meaning of the great comedies is that of an uproarious communion between the public and the play, a communion so chaotic that whole scenes of silliness and violence lead us almost to think that some of the 'rowdies' from the pit have climbed over the footlights. The title 'As You Like It', is, of course, an expression of utter carelessness, but it is not the bitter carelessness which Mr. Bernard Shaw fantastically reads into it; it is the god-like and inexhaustible carelessness of a happy man. And the simple proof of this is that there are scores of these genially taunting titles scattered through the whole of Elizabethan comedy. Is 'As You Like It' a title demanding a dark and ironic explanation in a school of comedy which called its plays 'What you Will', 'A Mad World, My Masters', 'If It Be Not Good, the Devil Is In It', 'The Devil is an Ass', 'An Humorous Day's Mirth', and 'A Midsummer Night's Dream'? Every one of these titles is flung at the head of the public as a drunken lord might fling a purse at his footman. Would Mr. Shaw maintain that 'If it Be Not Good, the Devil Is In It', was the opposite of 'As You Like It', and was a solemn invocation of the supernatural powers to testify to the care and perfection of the literary workmanship? The one explanation is as Elizabethan as the other.

Now in the reason for this modern and pedantic error lies the whole secret and difficulty of such plays as *A Midsummer Night's Dream.* The sentiment of such a play, so far as it can be summed up at all, can be summed up in one sentence. It is the mysticism of happiness. That is to say, it is the conception that as man lives upon a borderland he may find himself in the spiritual or supernatural atmosphere, not only through being profoundly sad or meditative, but by being extravagantly happy. The soul might be rapt out of the body in an agony of sorrow, or a trance of ecstasy; but it might also be rapt out of the body in a paroxysm of laughter. Sorrow we know can go beyond itself; so, according to Shakespeare, can pleasure go beyond itself and become something dangerous and unknown. And the reason that the logical and destructive modern school, of which Mr. Bernard Shaw is an example, does not grasp this purely exuberant nature of the comedies is simply that their logical and destructive attitude have rendered impossible the very experience of this preternatural exuberance. We cannot realize *As You Like It* if we are always considering it as we understand it. We cannot have *A Midsummer Night's Dream* if our one object in life is to keep ourselves awake with the black coffee of criticism. The whole question which is balanced, and balanced nobly and fairly, in *A Midsummer Night's Dream,* is whether the life of waking, or the life of the vision, is the real life, the *sine qua non* of man. But it is difficult to see what superiority for the purpose of judging is possessed by people whose pride it is not to live the life of vision at all. At least it is questionable whether the Elizabethan did not know more about both worlds than the modern intellectual; it is not altogether improbable that Shakespeare would not only have had a clearer vision of the fairies, but would have shot very much straighter at a deer and netted much more money for his performances than a member of the Stage Society.

In pure poetry and the intoxication of words, Shakespeare never rose higher than he rises in this play. But in spite of this fact, the supreme literary merit of *A Midsummer Night's Dream* is a merit of design. The amazing symmetry, the amazing artistic and moral beauty of that design, can be stated very briefly. The story opens in the sane and common world with the pleasant seriousness of very young lovers and very young friends. Then, as the figures advance into the tangled wood of young troubles and stolen happiness, a change and bewilderment begins to fall on them. They lose their way and their wits for they are in the heart of fairyland. Their words, their hungers, their very figures grow more and more dim and fantastic, like dreams within dreams, in the supernatural mist of Puck. Then the dream-fumes begin to clear and characters and spectators begin to awaken together to the noise of horns and dogs and the clean and bracing morning. Theseus, the incarnation of a happy and generous rationalism, expounds in hackneyed and superb lines the sane view of such psychic experiences, pointing out with a reverent and sympathetic scepticism that all these fairies and spells are themselves but the emanations, the unconscious masterpieces, of man himself. The whole company falls back into a splendid human laughter. There is a rush for banqueting and private theatricals, and over all these things ripples one of those frivolous and inspired conversations in which every good saying seems to die in giving birth to another. If ever the son of a man in his wanderings was at home and drinking by the fireside, he is at home in the house of Theseus. All the dreams have been forgotten, as a melancholy dream remembered throughout the morning might be forgotten in the human certainty of any other triumphant evening party; and so the play seems naturally ended. It began on the earth and it ends on the earth. Thus to round off the whole midsummer night's dream in an eclipse of daylight is an effect of genius. But of this comedy, as I have said, the mark is that genius goes beyond itself; and one touch is added which makes the play colossal. Theseus and his train retire with a crashing finale, full of humour and wisdom and things set right, and silence falls on the house. Then there comes a faint sound of little feet, and for a moment, as it were, the elves look into the house, asking which is the reality. 'Suppose we are the realities and they the shadows.' If that ending were acted properly any modern man would feel shaken to his marrow if he had to walk home from the theatre through a country lane.

—G. K. Chesterton, *"A Midsummer Night's Dream"* (1904), *G. K. Chesterton: A Selection from his Non-fictional Prose,* ed. W. H. Auden (London: Faber & Faber, 1970), pp. 92–95

G. WILSON KNIGHT ON THE DIVERSITY OF FAIRYLAND

[G. Wilson Knight (1897–1985), a leading British Shakespeare scholar, taught drama and English literature at the University of Leeds. He was the author of many volumes of criticism, including *The Starlit Dome* (1941), *The Crown of Life* (1947), and *Shakespeare and Religion* (1967). In this extract from *The Shakespearian Tempest* (1932), Knight asserts that the fairyland depicted in *A Midsummer Night's Dream* is a varied place full of both delights and dangers.]

In *A Midsummer Night's Dream* all the best of Shakespeare's earlier poetry is woven into so comprehensive and exquisite a design that it is hard not to feel that this play alone is worth all the other romances. We have observed plays where 'ill-dispersing' tempests are associated or contrasted with magic lands of fun, reunion, and final happiness. The happier elements of these plays are most perfectly embodied in Feste, song and comedy entwined, and perhaps this is why *Twelfth Night* appears so exquisite a flowering of humour and romance. Tempests and merchants, gold, jewels, and music are recurrent. But, whether love's setting be Arden, Ephesus, Belmont, or Illyria, we know that it is in reality a land of purely fanciful delight, a fairyland of successful, tempest-vanquishing romance. 'Illyria' is, indeed, more truly 'Elysium'. Yet such must be clearly related to those other images where, in the Histories and Early Tragedies, amid more realistic and tragic stress, the poet makes fleeting suggestion of the soul's desire set beyond rough seas of disaster and disorder, fairy riches on far-off Indian strands of the soul. Here we are actually introduced to this Indian fairyland; or, rather, the fairies have come from their Indian home to the 'wood near Athens' which is our scene. In this play fairyland interpenetrates the world of human action. And that world is varied, ranging from the rough simplicity of the clowns, through the solid common sense and kind worldly wisdom of Theseus, to the frenzied fantasies of the lovers: which in their turn shade into fairyland itself. The play thus encloses remarkably a whole scale of intuitions. Nor in any other early romance is the interplay of imagery more exqui-sitely varied. The night is a-glimmer with moon and star, yet it is dark and fearsome; there are gentle birds and gruesome beasts. There is a gnomish, fearsome, Macbeth-like quality about the atmosphere, just touching nightmare: yet these fairies are the actualization of Shakespeare's Indian dream. The total result resembles those dreams, of substance unhappy to the memorizing intellect, which yet, on waking, we find our-selves strangely regretting, loath to part from that magic even when it leaves nothing to the memory but incidents which should be painful. Such are the fairies here. They are neither good nor bad. They are wayward spirits which cause trouble to men, yet also woo human love and favour: as when Oberon and Titania quarrel for their Indian boy or wrangle in jealousy of Theseus or Hippolyta. The whole vision sums and expresses, as does no other work, the magic and the mystery of sleep, the dewy sweetness of a midsummer dream, dawn-memoried with sparkling grass and wreathing mists; a morning slope falling from a glade where late the moonbeams glimmered their fairy light on shadowed mossy boles and fearsome dells, and the vast woodland silence.

—G. Wilson Knight, *The Shakespearian Tempest* (London: Oxford University Press, 1932), pp. 141–42

❖

HAROLD C. GODDARD ON IMAGINATION IN *A MIDSUMMER NIGHT'S DREAM*

[Harold C. Goddard (1878–1950) was for many years head of the English department at Swarthmore College. He was the author of *Studies in New England Transcendentalism* (1906) and the editor of an edition of Ralph Waldo Emerson's essays (1926). In this extract, taken from his important book, *The Meaning of Shakespeare* (1951), Goddard explores the imaginative and dreamlike qualities of *A Midsummer Night's Dream*.]

A Midsummer-Night's Dream is itself, as its title says, a dream. Its action occurs mostly at night. Its atmosphere is that of moonlight and shadows. Its characters are forever falling asleep and dreaming. And at the end Puck invites the audience to believe that as they have been sitting there they have nodded and slumbered and that all that has passed before them has been a vision.

But as the other part of its title suggests, *A Midsummer-Night's Dream* is not only a dream, it is "play" in the quite literal sense of that term, a piece pervaded with the atmosphere of innocent idleness and joy befitting a midsummer night. It is not merely a play; it is the spirit of play in its essence. From the pranks of Puck and the frolics of the fairies, through the hide-and-seek of the lovers in the wood and the rehearsals of the rustics, on to the wedding festivities of the court and the final presentation of the masque of Pyramus and Thisbe, the tone of the piece is that of love-in-idleness, of activity for the sheer fun of it and for its own sake.

And because *A Midsummer-Night's Dream* is permeated with this spirit of doing things just for the love of doing them or for the love of the one for whom they are done, because the drama opens and closes on the wedding note and what comes between is just an interweaving of love stories, the piece may be said to be not only *dream* from end to end, and *play* from end to end, but also *love* from end to end.

And finally *A Midsummer-Night's Dream* is *art* from end to end—not just a work of art itself, which of course it is, but dedicated in good measure to the theme of art and made up of many little works of art of varying degrees of merit: its innumerable songs, its perpetual references to music, its rehearsal and presentation of the story of Pyramus and Thisbe, to say nothing of its many quotable passages, which, like the one about the hounds, the one about the superiority of silence to eloquence, the one about true love, the one about the mermaid on the dolphin's back, when lifted from their context seem like poems or pictures complete in themselves, whatever subtler values they may have in relation to the whole.

Dream, play, love, art. Surely it is no coincidence that these four "subjects" which are here interwoven with such consummate polyphony represent the four main aspects under which Imagination reveals itself in human life. Dream: what is that but a name for the world out of which man emerges into conscious life, the world of the unconscious as we have a habit of calling it today? Play: the instrument by which the child instinctively repeats the experience of the race and so by rehearsal prepares himself for the drama of life. Love: a revelation to each of the sexes that it is but a fragment of Another, which, by combined truth and illusion, seems at first concentrated in a person of the opposite sex. Art: the dream become conscious of itself, play grown to an adult estate, love freed of its illusion and transferred to wider and higher than personal ends. Dream, play, love, art: these four. Is there a fifth?

The fifth perhaps is what we finally have in this play, a union of the other four, Imagination in its quintessence—not just dream, nor play, nor love, nor art, but something above and beyond them all. With the attainment of it, the first becomes last, dream comes full circle as Vision, an immediate conscious apprehension of an invisible world, or, if you will, transubstantiation of the world of sense into something beyond itself.

The example of Bottom and his transformation will serve to bring these un-Shakespearean abstractions back to the concrete. To the average reader, Puck and Bottom are probably the most memorable characters in the play, Bottom especially. This instinct is right. Bottom is as much the master-character here as Launce is in *The Two Gentlemen of Verona*. Bottom symbolizes the earthy, the ponderous, the slow, in contrast with Puck, who is all that is quick, light, and aerial. Bottom is substance, the real in the common acceptation of that term. If Puck is the apex, Bottom is the base without whose four-square foundation the pyramid of life would topple over. He is the antithesis of the thesis of the play, the ballast that keeps the elfin bark of it from capsizing. He is literally what goes to the bottom. Like all heavy things he is content with his place in life, but his egotism is the unconscious selfishness of a child, both a sense and a consequence of his own individuality, not greed but pride in the good significance of that word. His realistic conception of stagecraft is in character. To Puck, Bottom is an ass. Yet Titania falls in love with him, ass's head and all.

> And I will purge thy mortal grossness so
> That thou shalt like an airy spirit go,

she promises. And she keeps her promise by sending him Bottom's dream.

The moment when Bottom awakens from this dream is the supreme moment of the play. There is nothing more wonderful in the poet's early works and few things more wonderful in any of them. For what Shakespeare has caught here in perfection is the original miracle of the Imagination, the awakening of spiritual life in the animal man. Bottom is an ass. If Bottom can be redeemed, matter itself and man in all his materiality can be redeemed also. Democracy becomes possible. Nothing less than this is what this incident implies. Yet when it is acted, so far as my experience in the theater goes, this divine insight is reduced to nothing but an occasion for roars of laughter. Laughter of course there should be, but laughter shot through with a beauty and pathos close to tears. Only an actor of genius could do justice to it. Bottom himself best indicates its quality when he declares that the dream deserves to be *sung* at the conclusion of a play and that it should be called Bottom's dream "because it hath no bottom." It is the same thought that Thoreau expounds when he shows why men persist in believing in bottomless ponds. For a moment in this scene, however far over the horizon, we sense the Shakespeare who was to describe the death of Falstaff, compose *King Lear,* and create Caliban.

Indeed, *A Midsummer-Night's Dream* as a whole is prophetic, in one respect at least, as is no other of the earlier plays, of the course the poet's genius was to take. There are few more fruitful ways of regarding his works than to think of them as an account of the warfare between Imagination and Chaos—or, if you will, between Imagination and the World—the story of the multifarious attempts of the divine faculty in man to ignore, to escape, to outwit, to surmount, to combat, to subdue, to forgive, to convert, to redeem, to transmute into its own substance, as the case may be, the powers of disorder that possess the world. Taken retrospectively, *A Midsummer-Night's Dream* seems like the argument of this story, like an overture to the vast musical composition which the poet's later masterpieces make up, like a seed from which the Shakespearean flower developed and unfolded.

—Harold C. Goddard, *The Meaning of Shakespeare* (Chicago: University of Chicago Press, 1951), pp. 78–80

C. L. Barber on Folk Mythology in *A Midsummer Night's Dream*

[C. L. Barber is the author of *The Whole Journey: Shakespeare's Power of Development* (1986) and *Shakespeare's Festive Comedy* (1959), from which the following extract is taken. Here, Barber comments on the humor of *A Midsummer Night's Dream* and Shakespeare's use of folk mythology in the creation of the setting and the spirits.]

Ovidian fancies pervade *A Midsummer Night's Dream,* and especially the scene of the fairy quarrel: the description of the way Cupid "loos'd his love shaft" at Elizabeth parallels the Metamorphoses' account of the god's shooting "his best arrow, with the golden head" at Apollo; Helena, later in the scene, exclaims that "The story shall be chang'd: / Apollo flies, and Daphne holds the chase"—and proceeds to invert animal images from Ovid. The game was not so much to lift things gracefully from Ovid as it was to make up fresh things in Ovid's manner, as Shakespeare here, by playful mythopoesis, explains the bad weather by his fairies' quarrel and makes up a metamorphosis of the little Western flower to motivate the play's follies and place Elizabeth superbly above them. The pervasive Ovidian influence accounts for Theseus' putting fables and fairies in the same breath when he says, punning on ancient and antic,

> I never may believe
> These antique fables nor these fairy toys. (V.i.2–3)

The humor of the play relates superstition, magic and passionate delusion as "fancy's images." The actual title emphasizes a sceptical attitude by calling the comedy a "dream." It seems unlikely that the title's characterization of the dream, "a midsummer night's dream," implies association with the specific customs of Midsummer Eve, the shortest night of the year, except as "midsummer night" would carry suggestions of a magic time. The observance of Midsummer Eve in England centered on building bonfires or "bonefires," of which there is nothing in Shakespeare's moonlight play. It was a time when maids might find out who their true love would be by dreams or divinations. There were customs of decking houses with greenery and hanging lights, which just possibly might connect with the fairies' torches at the comedy's end. And when people gathered fern seed at midnight, sometimes they spoke of spirits whizzing invisibly past. If one ranges through the eclectic pages of *The Golden Bough,* guided by the index for Midsummer Eve, one finds other customs suggestive of Shakespeare's play, involving moonlight, seeing the moon in water, gathering dew, and so on, but in Sweden, Bavaria, or still more remote places, rather than England. One can assume that parallel English customs have been lost, or one can assume that Shakespeare's imagination found its way to similarities with folk cult, starting from the custom of Maying and the general feeling that spirits may be abroad in the long dusks and short nights of midsummer. Olivia in *Twelfth Night* speaks of "midsummer madness" (III.iv.61). In the absence of evidence, there is no way to settle just how much comes from tradition. But what *is* clear is that Shakespeare was not *simply* writing out folklore which he heard in his youth, as Romantic critics liked to assume. On the contrary, his fairies are produced by a complex fusion of pageantry and popular game, as well as popular fancy. Moreover, as we shall see, they are not serious in the menacing way in which the people's fairies were serious. Instead they are serious in a very different way, as embodiments of the May-game experience of eros in men and women and trees and flowers, while any superstitious tendency to believe in their literal reality is mocked. The whole night's action is presented as a release of shaping fantasy which brings clarification about the tricks of strong imagination. We watch a dream; but we are awake, thanks to pervasive humor about the tendency to take fantasy literally, whether in love, in superstition, or in Bottom's mechanical dramatics. As in *Love's Labour's Lost* the folly of wit becomes the generalized comic subject in the course of a more inclusive release of imagination, the folly of fantasy becomes the general subject, echoed back and forth between the strains of the play's imitative counterpoint.

—C. L. Barber, *Shakespeare's Festive Comedy: A Study of Dramatic Form and Its Relation to Social Custom* (Princeton: Princeton University Press, 1959), pp. 122–24

BERTRAND EVANS ON OBERON AS A DRAMATIC FORCE

[Bertrand Evans (b. 1912) is the author of *Gothic Drama from Walpole to Shelley* (1947) and *Shakespeare's Tragic Practice* (1979). In this extract from *Shakespeare's Comedies* (1960), Evans explores the use of Oberon, the fairy king, as a dramatic force that influences the mortal characters.]

In *A Midsummer-Night's Dream,* for the first time, Shakespeare uses an 'outside force' which interferes in and controls the affairs of men. Oberon moves unseen, unheard, and unsuspected to the solution of the sole problem of the play (so far as the mortals are concerned)—that of restoring Demetrius's love to Helena. Although he differs in form and nature from

Shakespeare's later notable forces of control as markedly as they differ from one another, the fairy king is like them all both in his essential dramatic function and in the attributes which enable him to perform this function—superior power and superior awareness. Like the Fate that operates throughout *Romeo and Juliet* (according to the Prologue) and the Fate of which the witches are the visible figureheads in *Macbeth,* but unlike Duke Vincentio in *Measure for Measure* and Prospero in *The Tempest,* Oberon is supernatural and immortal. Like Vincentio and Prospero, and unlike Fate in the tragedies, he is benevolent. Like Fate itself and unlike the others, he remains always invisible to the mortal participants—but, unlike Fate, he is visible to us. Like all the others except the Fate of *Romeo and Juliet,* he makes observable contact with mortals, either directly or through an intermediary. Also like all the others except the Fate of *Romeo and Juliet,* he requires special aids or 'props' in wielding his power. Unlike all the others, he is concerned quite incidentally with the affairs of mortals. And, finally, he falls a little short of the others' omniscience and omnipotence: under his direction things can temporarily get out of hand.

Although he has come on purpose to bless the bed of Theseus and Hippolyta, Oberon's interference in the dilemma of the four Athenian youths comes about by chance. The juice of the flower for which he sends Puck was meant only for Titania's eyes, to compel her to surrender her little changeling boy. It is while he awaits Puck's return that Demetrius and Helena enter, quarrelling. 'I am invisible,' says the fairy king, 'and I will overhear their conference.' The 'conference' of the angry young man and the hurt and bitter maid runs through fifty-six lines and represents the play's first use of a discrepancy between the participants' vision and ours: the couple are ignorant by what immortal eye they are being watched. When they have gone, Oberon speaks:

> Fare thee well, nymph. Ere he do leave this grove,
> Thou shalt fly him and he shall seek thy love.

Neither now nor ever after are Helena and Demetrius—or, indeed, any of the other human participants—to know that a force from outside their mortal circle has looked on their affairs, apprehended their dilemma, and interceded in the cause of true love. From this first point on, a gap divides the human participants' view from ours. This gap is unique in Shakespeare's comedies in that it remains open even at the end of the play. We alone know that an immortal spirit has manipulated human events and solved a mortal problem.

Immortal, yet not quite omniscient: 'Anoint his eyes,' says Oberon to Puck,

> But do it when the next thing he espies
> May be the lady. Thou shalt know the man
> By the Athenian garments he hath on.   (II. i. 261–4.)

'Fear not, my lord,' replies Puck, 'your servant shall do so.' But even as Oberon gives these directions, we know, since the dramatist has taken care to advise us, that not one but two young men in Athenian garments are in the forest. Having seen only Demetrius, and being preoccupied with Titania, Oberon does not foresee the possibility of error. From this point until well into III. ii our Olympian perch is set not only above mortals but above immortals also. Dutifully seeking out a youth in Athenian weeds, and finding Lysander and Hermia sleeping far apart on the ground, as Hermia's sense of propriety has required, fallible Puck concludes that these are the estranged mortals who must be made to love each other. 'Believe me, king of shadows, I mistook', he asserts later, when he and Oberon discover what abuse their errors have wrought. Puck errs because Oberon erred in directing him, and thus, though the ultimate cause is the magical juice of the little western flower, the immediate cause of the comic action involving the lovers is a blunder made because immortal intelligence has fallen, for once, a little short of omniscience.
　　　　—Bertrand Evans, *Shakespeare's Comedies* (Oxford: Clarendon Press, 1960), pp. 34–36

[John Dover Wilson (1881–1969), formerly the Regius Professor of Education at King's College at the University of London, was a noted Shakespeare scholar. Among his works are *What Happens in* Hamlet (1935), *The Meaning of* The Tempest (1936), and *Shakespeare's Happy Comedies* (1962), from which the following extract is taken. Here, Wilson comments on some of the structural points of *A Midsummer Night's Dream,* including the role of Puck.]

The play has been justly praised for its ingenuity. It consists in fact of four plots so cleverly intertwined that the working of each is necessary for the working of the others, the cusp, if I may so call it, at which the lines of the tracery meet being Cupid's little magic flower. What is technically the main or central plot is provided by the Lovers who form the usual quartet that we find at the centre of most of the Happy Comedies: two men and two women at cross purposes, Lysander and Hermia being the true-loves, Demetrius the unfaithful man and Helena the forlorn lady. Here however the imbroglio that holds up the happy ending is the result not of confused identity arising from a family resemblance or an assumed disguise, but of supernatural intervention by Puck, who brings it about by the mistaken application of Cupid's flower and in the end resolves it by means of its antidote, Dian's bud. This pivot of the lovers' plot is pivot also of the Fairies', since it is to punish Titania that Oberon sends for Cupid's flower in the first place. Further the plot of the Mechanicals turns on it as well; for it is by dropping the magic juice into her eyes that Oberon causes the fairy queen to fall in love with Bottom, while the plot of Bottom and his fellow mechanicals is linked with the plot that envelops the whole play, the marriage of Duke Theseus, since they meet in the wood to prepare for that marriage. Finally, the marriage itself is doubly linked with the Lovers' plot, first by the Duke's command to Hermia to conform to her father's will and consent to marry Demetrius within the next four days; and secondly by the Lovers, now sorted out, being married themselves at the same time as the Duke. Thus the plot mechanism has a circular as well as a transverse motion. No plot by Ben Jonson is more cunning, and more successfully concealed; for all that the audience is aware of is the inevitable sequence of the events it produces. But while Jonson's plots work towards the confounding or exposure of his chief characters, Shakespeare's find their consummation in happiness. And none of his comic consummations is neater or happier than this. For with supernatural characters at his disposal Shakespeare can make them intervene at any point he chooses. And he is able as well to bring the Fairies back at the end to give us that ravishing epilogue in which they sing the three pairs of married lovers to bed and bestow upon them, and upon us the audience, their blessing.

—John Dover Wilson, *Shakespeare's Happy Comedies* (Evanston, IL: Northwestern University Press, 1962), pp. 185–86

ROBERT W. DENT ON THE NATURE OF LOVE IN *A MIDSUMMER NIGHT'S DREAM*

[Robert W. Dent (b. 1917), formerly a professor of English at the University of California at Los Angeles, is the author of *John Webster's Borrowing* (1960) and *Shakespeare's Proverbial Language: An Index* (1980). In this extract, Dent examines the structural and thematic use of the lovers in *A Midsummer Night's Dream*.]

Nothing is more common than the observation that *A Midsummer Night's Dream* is a play "about love", about lovers' lunacy, where "reason and love keep little company together nowadays", where the follies of imagination-dominated Demetrius and Lysander are reduced to their essential absurdity by the passion of Titania for an ass. It is for the sake of this theme, surely, that Demetrius and Lysander are given so little distinctive characterization; they cannot contrast like a Claudius and a Benedick, so that a particular pairing of lovers is demanded by the characters of those involved. For the same reason, paradoxically, Hermia and Helena are differentiated, to heighten the puzzle of love's choices (as well as to increase the potentialities for comedy in the play's middle). By all conventional Elizabethan standards, tall fair gentle Helena should be the one pursued, and when Lysander eventually boasts his use of reason in preferring a dove to a raven his argument, by those standards, is indeed rational. Our laughter stems from recognizing that it is so only accidentally, as rationalization.

According to a good many critics, Shakespeare contrasts from the start the irrationality of the lovers with what these critics regard as the admirable rationality of Theseus-Hippolyta. The latter become a kind of ideal which the lovers approach by the end of the play. If so, the role of imagination in love is simple and obvious; it is a disrupting irrational influence which must eventually be purged, and will prove in simple and total contrast to the disciplined use of imagination essential to Shakespeare's art. But I cannot see that any contrast so mechanical as this is intended.

When, thanks to Dian's bud, Lysander returns to Hermia, his "true love", the return marks a release from dotage but no return to reason as such, any more than does Demetrius' return to Helena by the pansy-juice. Love's choices remain inexplicable, and the eventual pairings are determined only by the constancy of Helena and Hermia in their initial inexplicable choices. As so frequently in Shakespearian comedy, the men fluctuate before finally settling down to a constant attachment such as the heroines exhibit from the start. Men's "fancies are more giddy and unfirm, / More longing, wavering, sooner lost and won, / Than women's are" ⟨Twelfth Night⟩. In the case of true love, once stabilized—even as in the case of mere dotage—imagination cannot "form a shape, / Besides yourself to like of" ⟨The Tempest⟩; it "carries no favour in't" but that of the beloved ⟨All's Well That Ends Well⟩. Unlike dotage, however, it is in no obvious conflict with reason, either in its object or its vehemence. By the end of the fourth act we are assured that Demetrius and Lysander have come to stability of this kind. But the terminus, I repeat, is not a rationally determined one. Like Theseus at the play's beginning, at the play's ending Demetrius and Lysander are settled. Jill has Jack, nought shall go back, and the prospect of happy marriage is before them all.

Thus in *A Midsummer Night's Dream* the origin of love never lies in reason. Love may be consistent with reason—e.g., Lysander is undeniably "a worthy gentleman"—and a healthy imagination, although influenced by love, will not glaringly rebel against reason. But as Hermia initially indicates, her choice is dictated not by her judgment but by her "eyes", by the vision of Lysander as her love-dictated imagination reports it. As Helena says at the close of this same introductory scene, love sees with that part of the mind that has no taste of judgment. Essentially this is as true for Hermia as for the others, although her choice conflicts with parental authority rather than with sound evaluation of her beloved's merits. Despite Egeus' initial disapproval, nevertheless, her choice is eventually confirmed. She is not compelled to "choose love by another's eyes" (I. i. 140), to see with her father's judgment (as Theseus at first demanded; I. i. 57), nor even to convert her love to one directed by her own judgment. Her love at the end is what it was at the beginning, with the obstacles removed.

Not even Egeus accuses her of dotage, although he does think her somehow "witched" in her refusal to accept his choice rather than her own. "Dotage", in this play, appears essentially reserved for two kinds of amorous excess approaching madness: the monomaniacal pursuit of an unrequited love (thus Helena "dotes in idolatry", Demetrius "dotes" on Hermia's eyes, and Lysander dotes for Helena in the night's comedy of errors), or the ridiculous bestowal of affection upon an obviously unworthy object (most grotesquely in Titania's passion for Bottom, but also in the gross excesses of Lysander and Demetrius during their "dream").

In the middle of the play, then, when dotage grows most rampant, so too does imagination. The frenzied praises and dispraises of Lysander and Demetrius are exceeded only by Titania's infatuation for Bottom, her hearing beauty in his voice, seeing beauty in his ears, and so on. Were follies so excessive in the cases of the mortal lovers, we could never end as we do in marriage and lasting love. Yet by the end of Act IV, with all obstacles to happily paired marriages removed—no thanks to the behavior of the lovers—the lovers can sound, and behave, rationally enough. Their love, however, is in its essence as inexplicable as ever.

The inexplicability of love's choices was of course a favorite topic for discussion in the age and a favorite theme for Shakespearian comedy. Why should two particular people fall in love, often at first sight? Were they so destined by the stars, like Romeo and Juliet (but not Romeo and Rosaline)? Were they marked by peculiarly "correspondent qualyties of bloud"?

To this question *A Midsummer Night's Dream* perhaps suggests no kind of answer beyond the fact that such true loves do exist, are distinct from the fancy-dominated aberrations that mark inconstancy, and when properly terminating in marriage are part of the natural—and, in that sense, rational—order of things. From the start of the play, the mystery of love's choices (including the attendant male inconstancies) is stressed. Egeus, at least metaphorically, thinks Hermia "witched", and all Elizabethans would be reminded of disputes on whether love could be caused by witchcraft, or by philtres and charms, whether naturally or supernaturally administered. When the fairies first appear (in II. i), and before ever they become involved with the lovers, Shakespeare skillfully prepares us for their role. First, the inexplicable fortunes and misfortunes of housewives are attributed to Puck—this may well receive first mention because it is drawn from folklore, is familiar to the audience, and thus allows the easiest transition into what follows. A few lines later, all the recently experienced disorders of the English-Athenian weather are similarly attributed to temporary discord in the fairy macrocosm:

> And this same progeny of evils comes
> From our debate, from our dissension.   (II. i. 115–116)

For this night on which we can see fairies, we are allowed to understand, playfully, the cause for otherwise unaccountable phenomena. It is in such a context, too, that we hear the play's only reference to Theseus' well known infidelities preceding his "true love" marriage to Hippolyta; these too are charged to fairy influence (although Titania discounts the charge). In short, aspects of the inexplicable past, familiar to the audience, have been imaginatively explained as fairy-caused.

—Robert W. Dent, "Imagination in *A Midsummer Night's Dream*," *Shakespeare Quarterly* 15, No. 2 (Spring 1964): 116–18

STEPHEN FENDER ON SHAKESPEARE'S DEVELOPMENT OF CHARACTER

[Stephen Fender is a professor at the University of Edinburgh in Scotland. He is the author of *English Renaissance Literature: Introductory Essays* (1974) and *Sea Changes: British Emigration and American Literature* (1992). In this extract from his study of *A Midsummer Night's Dream*, Fender explores Shakespeare's development of character in the play.]

It may be that many, if not most, of the over-simple interpretations of *A Midsummer Night's Dream* stem from a failure to understand the way in which Shakespeare develops the characters in the play. Anyone expecting the kind of 'true-to-life' subtlety of personality with which Shakespeare endows characters in the other comedies will be disappointed at the thinness of detail in the 'personalities' of Hermia, Helena, Lysander, and Demetrius. Indeed the assumption is not uncommon that *A Midsummer Night's Dream* relates to the later comedies as a sort of apprentice piece, the play in which Shakespeare learned the techniques of developing 'fully rounded' characters which he was later to perfect in, say, *As You Like It*. This assumption may well explain the tendency to simplify the play (and the corresponding need to fantasticate it with spectacle and machinery), since anyone looking for richness of realistic detail and not finding it may be excused for underrating the complexity of what is left without it. The complexity of the play certainly does not consist in subtle distinctions of individual personalities, but before establishing the rather special nature of the play's difficulty, we must attempt to clear the air around this problem of 'character'.

The (obvious enough) fact is that when we talk of 'character' in *A Midsummer Night's Dream,* we mean something so radically different from 'character' in the other comedies that the play cannot usefully be considered as a stage in Shakespeare's development as a portrayer of fully rounded characters at all. In *As You Like It* (a useful contrast because the plot is very roughly similar to that of *A Midsummer Night's Dream*) Rosalind and Orlando, Jaques, Celia, even Duke Senior are all recognisable as individuals, each with his own 'character'. With the exception of Silvius and Hymen, no character in *As You Like It* could be called a 'type'; no one 'stands for' anything. Indeed much of the interest of the play is focused on how these clearly individualised characters develop, and Orlando's education in the process of true love is thematically central. On the other hand, after reading or watching *A Midsummer Night's Dream* we have the greatest difficulty in remembering for long even important details about the characters. Which of the girls is forbidden by her father to marry which of the men? Who is the tall girl, and who is the short one? Who marries whom at the end? Their names seem little more than labels, as interchangeable as their alliances in the wood.

Indeed, with the exception of Bottom, 'character' in the play is not so much developed as defined:

> *Fairy:* Either I mistake your shape and making quite,
> Or else you are that shrewed and knavish sprite
> Called Robin Goodfellow. Are not you he
> That frights the maidens of the villagery,
> Skim milk, and sometimes labour in the quern,
> And bootless make the breathless housewife churn,
> And sometimes make the drink to bear no barm,
> Mislead night-wanderers, laughing at their harm?
> Those that 'Hobgoblin' call you, and 'Sweet Puck',
> You do their work, and they shall have good luck.
> Are you not he?
> *Puck:*   Thou speakest aright:
> I am that merry wanderer of the night.   (II. i)

This exchange sounds about as natural as the beginning of a music-hall routine (with 'Fairy' playing the straight man); it is crude, intrusive exposition written largely in end-stopped lines—reminiscent (or so it seems at first) of the 'early Shakespeare' of *Henry VI*. But there is an important difference: in *A Midsummer Night's Dream* certain passages in which the dialogue seems unrealistic are used deliberately, for specific effects. Elsewhere in the play the dialogue is 'natural' enough, in Act V, for example, or at the end of Act IV; but in passages which delineate character, as well as in some of the lovers' remarks in the wood, which we will examine later, Shakespeare chooses a more formal, even stilted style. In the case of Puck's introduction and first speech, the formal style suits the way his 'character' is presented: he is not allowed to develop into an individual with his own unique style. Instead he is described—in the first instance by someone else—according to certain traditional modes of behaviour. The passage reminds us (and might have reminded the play's original audience) of one of those Renaissance dictionaries that described mythological and legendary figures by a brief résumé of their lives and according to the moral values they presented. The only difference is that here the subject is the 'mythology' of English folk-lore, not of antiquity. ⟨. . .⟩

In *A Midsummer Night's Dream,* then, Shakespeare defines his characters according to what they represent, according to their labels. The lovers are not individuals, they are 'lovers', and the definition of that word will determine their behaviour; Puck's actions too are predicated by the definition of 'Puck'. Nor is the process restricted to characters; even places stand for something, are labels. Athens, established in literary tradition as the legendary seat of reason (in Boccaccio's *Teseida* and 'The Knight's Tale') is here almost a byword for rational order. The wilderness outside Athens is called a 'wood' and not a forest, as is the corresponding locale in *As You Like It,* because it must also be a label for 'mad', and in case we miss the point, Demetrius is made to pun on 'wood' (for 'mad' and 'forest') and 'wooed'; 'And here am I, and wood within this wood. . . .' With everything so clearly defined and with the infinite complexities of realistic character and 'real life' settings so firmly excised, no wonder those who came looking for realism go away convinced that the play is a little too simple.

—Stephen Fender, *Shakespeare: A* Midsummer Night's Dream (London: Edward Arnold, 1968), pp. 13–15, 20

JAMES E. ROBINSON ON SOME LITERARY INFLUENCES ON SHAKESPEARE

[James E. Robinson is a professor of English at the University of Notre Dame. In this extract, Robinson studies the sources from which Shakespeare inherited his ideas of comedy.]

A Midsummer Night's Dream concludes with a grand epithalamion in which several levels of society and the spirits of nature appear in festivity and celebration. Insofar as the play has proceeded in a magical context (the moonlit wood) with invocation of magical device (the personified spirits of love and their potions) to issue in celebration of the union of man and nature, it is processional, ceremonial, symbolical. In this sense it is comedy as ritual. And yet in the process the play has exposed folly and given perspective to love; it has interpreted human experience. In this sense it is comedy as argument, comedy as rhetoric. What I offer in this essay is an approach that attempts to comprehend the artistic method that underlies Shakespeare's fusion of these two comic ideas into the single apprehension that is the play. ⟨. . .⟩

Shakespeare and his age inherited the idea of ritualistic comedy in several ways. In Renaissance discussions of comedy, the idea was preserved in comments on the origin of comedy in ancient Greek times. William Webbe, for example, in *A Discourse of English Poetrie* (1586) explained that "Commedies tooke their name of κωμάζειν καὶ ᾄδειν, *commessatum ire*, to goe a feasting, because they vsed to goe in procession with their sport about the Citties and Villages, mingling much pleasaunt myrth wyth theyr graue Religion, and feasting cheerefully together wyth as great ioy as might be deuised." Similar kinds of ritualistic comic expression developed in England from Christian and primitive traditions. The mystery cycle plays performed on the Corpus Christi holiday affirmed belief in scriptural myth and, in total scope, celebrated the victory of resurrection and eternal destiny. The chapters in E. K. Chambers' *The Mediaeval Stage* on various kinds of folk drama, such as "Festival Play," "The May-Game," and "The Sword-Dance," present interesting testimony of the numerous forms of seasonal celebrations that developed in England out of primitive ritual. Speaking of the sword dances and the St. George plays, Chambers remarks that they are the "outcome of the instinct of play, manipulating for its own purposes the mock sacrifice and other débris of extinct ritual. Their central incident symbolizes the *renouveau,* the annual death of the year or the fertilization spirit and its annual resurrection in spring."

A second main tradition of comedy inherited by Shakespeare was based on the Roman comedy of Plautus and Terence. The plays of Plautus and Terence are set in the context of a specific social structure and a well-defined system of laws and mores. Typically, the desires of young men are placed in opposition to the more sober concerns of citizen fathers who are particularly adamant when the girls whom the young men pursue are not citizens of the Athenian world in which the plays are usually set. The clever servant, who should be obedient and keep his place, attempts to turn the social order upside down by out-witting the father and advancing the amour of the son. Specific problems arise if a slave owner objects to a young man's attempt to make off with a girl legally bound to the owner or if a son has incurred a debt against his father's wishes and knowl-edge. The plots are a series of moves and countermoves designed to maneuver the play's characters through social and legal complications to a point where a discovery or a stratagem allows conflicting parties to come together in a situation of awareness and agreement, a feast and a wedding promised as a celebration of the social concord. In the process a myopic father may be exposed as a foolish dotard, a braggart soldier as a bumptious pretender, a young lover as a sentimental dreamer, a wife as a shrew, a slave dealer as a villainous rascal. A parade of parasites, courtesans, domestics, and assorted citizens, each with a proper social role to play, fills out the stage of Roman comedy, the drama of everyday life.

The definition of this kind of comedy, a definition that became the major premise of the Renaissance conception of classical comedy, was articulated by Cicero in the oration *Pro Sexto Roscio Amerino.* Cicero referred to a situation in a Roman comedy to illustrate a point he was arguing, and then to affirm the cogency of the example, he said: "I think, in fact, that these fictions of the poets are intended to give us a repre-sentation of our manners in the character of others and a vivid picture of our daily life." Aelius Donatus, a fourth-century com-mentator, whose work on Terence was ubiquitously published, imitated, and expanded in the Renaissance, repeated Cicero's remark in substance as a definition of comedy in a prefatory essay to his commentary: "Cicero has said that comedy is an imitation of life, a mirror of custom, an image of truth."

It is significant that this definition originated with a rhetorician, for it accentuates the relation of rhetoric and comedy that became a central part of Renaissance literary criticism. From classical authorities the Renaissance inherited the idea that rhetoric was a form of art designed to give persuasive force to the truths of civilized life. For example, the author of the *Rhetorica ad Herennium,* a Roman rhetoric much admired in the Renaissance, said, "The task of the public speaker is to discuss capably those matters which law and custom have fixed for the uses of citizenship, and to secure as far as possible the agreement of his hearers." This emphasis on the social context and persuasive end of rhetoric was often paralleled by a similar emphasis placed on comedy in Renaissance criticism. Gregorius Wagnerus, a commentator on Terence, said, for example, "Set forth in individual comedies are certain definite propositions concerning the various manners, characters, and duties of men, propositions which do a great deal for the promotion of a wise and civilized life." Wagnerus then used the language of Cicero and Donatus referred to above to define comedy, and added: "Indeed, it [comedy] commends virtues and censures vices, and presents the substance of virtue in whatever kind of age, sex, and condition. We see here the image and vivid representation of almost all domestic actions."

This conception of comedy as an imitation of everyday life that functions as a kind of dramatic argument to dissuade men from vice and move them to virtue was a common one in the discussions of comedy by sixteenth-century English apologists of poetry. Because of the brevity and generality of their comments and because of the narrowly moralistic emphasis (not that the English were alone in this emphasis), the English theorists presented a limited conception of a rhetorical idea of comedy. Nevertheless they promoted such an idea by affirming the importance of the social context and persuasive end of comedy. Sidney, for example, emphasized the importance of the social context when he explained how the manner in which comedy handles "our priuate and domestical matters" can teach us in "the actions of our life" to know evil so as better to perceive virtue. He affirmed the persuasive effect of comedy in

his definition of the genre: "Comedy is an imitation of the common errors of our life, which he [the comic poet] representeth in the most ridiculous and scornefull sort that may be; so as it is impossible that any beholder can be content to be such a one."
—James E. Robinson, "The Ritual and Rhetoric of *A Midsummer Night's Dream*," *PMLA* 83, No. 2 (May 1968): 380–82

THOMAS MCFARLAND ON THE SETTING OF *A MIDSUMMER NIGHT'S DREAM*

[Thomas McFarland (b. 1926) is the author of *Tragic Meanings in Shakespeare* (1966), *Coleridge and the Pantheist Tradition* (1969), and *Shakespeare's Pastoral Comedy* (1972), from which the following extract is taken. Here, McFarland discusses the use of the setting—the "moonlit forest"—in *A Midsummer Night's Dream*.]

A Midsummer Night's Dream is the happiest of Shakespeare's plays, and very possibly the happiest work of literature ever conceived. The merriment of *Love's Labour's Lost* is here reaffirmed, but the formal artifice of that play, which may be indicated by the word "labour" in the title, transforms itself now into a frolic less formed and more evanescent, as indicated by the word "dream." The merry sport of the earlier play becomes less verbal and teasing, more graceful and moonlit. Honeysuckle diction now veils environment and action in a tone softer and more luxuriant. "The reading of this play," says Hazlitt, "is like wandering in a grove by moonlight: the descriptions breathe a sweetness like odours thrown from beds of flowers." It is the moment of pure pastoral celebration.

The play, indeed, almost stills the conflicts of drama to achieve the static completeness of a painting. "Part of the delight of this poetry," says C. L. Barber, "is that we can enjoy without agitation imaginative action of the highest order" (*Shakespeare's Festive Comedy*). The language is virtually one long celebration. The comic deviances are not only artificial, but casual. Where *Love's Labour's Lost* fabricates its deviances and turns itself into a game, *A Midsummer Night's Dream* moves in dreamlike sequences as if on the brink of an eternal bliss.

The setting, though nominally the Athens of myth and the woodland of dreams, is likewise a conflation of the sweetest aspects of the English countryside. And it is still further an unmistakable version of pastoral. As H. B. Charlton says in a notable passage:

> England's cowslips were golden cups, spotted with rich rubies, and a pearl of dew hung in each. The woodlands were carpeted with thick primrose beds, and its springtime outrivalled that of Theocritus in greenery: the song of the lark in the season when wheat is green and hawthorn buds appear, roused English villages betimes to do observances to the month of May. The fields are asparkle with the dewdrop's liquid pearl: the woods are lighted with the fiery glow-worm's eyes. Morning has mountain top and western valley filled with music of the hounds. . . . And evening ushers in the midnight revels on hill, in dale, forest or mead, by paved fountain or by rushy brook, or in the beached margent of the sea, where ringlets are danced in quaint mazes to the whistling of the wind. This is the land of *A Midsummer Night's Dream*. *(Shakespearian Comedy.)*

Even the golden sun is too harsh a light for this play's happiness; and the moon shining down on a midsummer's night makes the darkness not a condition of anxiety, but a symbol of soft and benign exhilaration.

Where *Love's Labour's Lost* enlists the power of its king in the formal deviance of withdrawal from women, the mightier ruler, Theseus, clothed in centuries of mythical association, declares from the beginning the existence of a state of comic and pastoral grace. The words that begin the play, "Now, fair Hippolyta, our nuptial hour / Draws on apace" (1.1.1–2), reveal that the ultimate social confirmation already obtains, and that, under its protection, nobody can come to harm. In the opening speeches other motifs of happiness are revealed one by one:

> four happy days bring in
> Another moon; but, O, methinks, how slow
> This old moon wanes! [1.1.2–4]

The play's first line establishes the mood of nuptial anticipation; the second, the reality of happy days; the third, the soft moonlight that will suffuse the action. The language of the bride-to-be, thus kindled, attains a silvery lightness:

> Four days will quickly steep themselves in night;
> Four nights will quickly dream away the time;
> And then the moon, like to a silver bow
> New-bent in heaven, shall behold the night
> Of our solemnities.   [1.1.7–11]

The anticipation of happiness in Hippolyta's lines, dreaming on things to come, is followed by Theseus's invocation of a similar bliss for society at large:

>   Go, Philostrate,
> Stir up the Athenian youth to merriments;
> Awake the pert and nimble spirit of mirth;   [1.1.11–13]

And he concludes, to Hippolyta, with words that decree the entire course of the play: "I will wed thee," he says—"With pomp, with triumph, and with revelling" (1.1.18–19).

It is difficult to imagine a comic opening to compare with this one in the benignity of its tone and in its absolute guarantee of gladness. The action of the play that follows can now be nothing other than a pretext for the continuing celebration of a joyous event, in a wondrous realm, in a timeless time.
—Thomas McFarland, *Shakespeare's Pastoral Comedy* (Chapel Hill: University of North Carolina Press, 1972), pp. 78–80

ALEXANDER LEGGATT ON SHAKESPEARE'S DRAMATIC TECHNIQUES

[Alexander Leggatt (b. 1940) is a professor of English at the University of Toronto and the author of *Citizen Comedy in the Age of Shakespeare* (1973) and

Shakespeare's Political Drama: The History Plays and the Roman Plays (1988). In this extract from *Shakespeare's Comedy of Love* (1974), Leggatt explores the way in which Shakespeare plays characters off one another for comic effect.]

If much of the play's comic life depends on playing different groups of characters off against each other, much of its power to haunt the imagination comes from its suggestion of the ultimate unity of the various worlds it depicts. In a variety of small touches, echoes are set up between one scene and another. Immediately after Hermia awakes in panic from a dream of being attacked by a serpent, we find the mechanicals engaged in taking the terror out of their play, to avoid frightening the ladies. The music and dance of the fairies are followed by the more robust music of the daylight world, the hounds and horns of Theseus; and at the end of *Pyramus and Thisbe* the clowns, like the fairies, show that they too can dance, in their own way. In the final scene, Theseus's earthy jokes about the couples' impatience to get to bed introduce an idea that is picked up and transformed by Oberon's celebration of fertility; just as in Puck's opening words, 'Now the hungry lion roars' (V. i. 360), Snug's apologetic performance sets off an unexpected echo from a more serious world. The various worlds of the play mirror each other, and are ultimately seen as one world, moving in a single rhythm. This feeling is particularly strong from the later forest scenes to the end of the play, as references to time accumulate, and the characters all feel caught in a common rhythm, moving from night into day, and then back again.

Just as each group of characters is placed against the others, so the artistic world they all form together is seen in relation to other kinds of experience, outside the normal scope of comedy. Throughout the play we are made aware of the process of selection by which the comic world is created. The process begins, simply enough, with Theseus's words in the opening scene, 'Turn melancholy forth to funerals; / The pale companion is not for our pomp' (I. i. 14–15). Puck and Oberon are careful to draw a distinction between themselves and the 'damned spirits' of the night, but in so doing they remind us of the existence of those spirits (III. ii. 378–95; V. i. 360–79).

61

Titania's lullaby invokes the slimy creeping things of the forest, telling them to keep their distance (II. ii. 9–24). Hermia's dream is frightening enough, but, as in other scenes with the lovers, the formal style with its rhyming couplets helps to cool the terror (II. ii. 145–56). Similarly, the suggestion of bestiality in Titania's affair with Bottom is kept under control by the cool, decorative poetry as she leads him off the stage:

> Come, wait upon him; lead him to my bower.
> The moon, methinks, looks with a wat'ry eye;
> And when she weeps, weeps every little flower,
> Lamenting some enforced chastity. (III. i. 182–5)

They are going off to bed, but there is nothing torrid about it. The forest might have been a place of unbridled eroticism, but it is not: Lysander and Hermia are very careful about their sleeping arrangements, and Demetrius warns Helena to keep away from him so as not to endanger her virginity (II. i. 214–19). Normally, couples going into the woods mean only one thing, but the lovers of this play are aware of the energies the forest might release, and determined to keep those energies under control. On the other hand the ideal of chastity, in Theseus's reference to Diana's nunnery and in Oberon's description of the imperial votaress who is immune to love, is set aside as something admirable but too high and remote for ordinary people. The play is aware of both extreme attitudes to sex, but steers a civilized middle course appropriate to comedy.

Other possible kinds of art are also referred to, and then banished. Theseus, selecting a play for his wedding night, rejects anything involving satire, eunuchs or the dismembering of poets (V. i. 44–55). Bottom and his crew try to perform a tragedy, and turn it into a glorious farce: the whole machinery of tragedy, Fates, Furies and all, disappears into laughter. More soberly, Oberon refers to some of the smaller miseries produced by the ordinary workings of nature, and banishes them:

> Never mole, hare-lip, nor scar,
> Nor mark prodigious, such as are
> Despised in nativity,
> Shall upon their children be. (V. i. 400–3)

Throughout the play, we seem to be witnessing a constant process of exorcism, as forces which could threaten the safety of the comic world are called up, only to be driven away. The play stakes out a special area of security in a world full of hostile forces: just as the mortal world is very close to the fairy world, yet finally separate from it, so the comic world of the play is very close to a darker world of passion, terror and chaos, yet the border between them, though thin, is never broken.

—Alexander Leggatt, *Shakespeare's Comedy of Love* (London: Methuen, 1974), pp. 109–11

RONALD E. MILLER ON SHAKESPEARE'S USE OF FAIRIES

[Ronald E. Miller is an American literary critic who, in this extract, studies the use of fairies in *A Midsummer Night's Dream,* including their origins in the Latin poet Ovid and in English folklore.]

The complex and subtle intellectuality of Shakespeare's comic art was never better illustrated than by *A Midsummer Night's Dream* and, in particular, by Shakespeare's employment of the fairies in that play. Not only are they obviously the most striking feature of the comedy; intellectually they are the most provocative, too. By intruding the fictive worlds of Ovid and English folklore into the doings of the nobles and the workmen of Athens, they pose open-ended questions about illusion and reality, existence and art to those willing to press beyond the older interpretation of the play as a charming theatrical fantasy or a comic medley or a burlesque. Such puzzles have occupied so much recent critical attention that this comedy, once rather generally dismissed as a piece of fluff, is now more likely to be read as a study in the epistemology of the imagination.

And this tendency seems justified. The fairies are a continual and unavoidable reminder of a certain indefiniteness in the world of the play—an indefiniteness culminating in the suggestion by the fairy prankster Puck that the play itself may have only been a dream: "If we shadows have offended, / Think but this, and all is mended, / That you have but slumb'red here / While these visions did appear" (V. i. 430–33). With that final insinuation, the frame of dramatic illusion is irreparably compromised, and little remains besides a series of tantalizing riddles. Are the fairies real or unreal? Are the spectators no less than the Athenians subject to Puck's and Oberon's magic? How can we assign precedence to the various levels of reality—including our own—under the sway of Shakespeare's art? Such doubts tease us into abstract thoughts as inescapable as their conclusions are elusive and uncertain.

The intellectual implications of the fairies, however, have scarcely been exhausted once the puzzle of their metaphysical status has been explored. No doubt there *is* a certain fugitiveness to these beings. Shakespeare lets us have our fairies and doubt them too. Yet beyond these formal uncertainties lie other uncertainties residing not in the world of the stage but in the world of ordinary human experience to which every dramatic representation, no matter how sophisticated, must ultimately refer. As theatrical immanences—ambulatory metaphors, if you wish—who secretly manipulate affections, cause transformations, and bring good luck, the fairies obliquely hint that our own offstage existence may be touched by mysteries no less genuine than those that disrupt the world of Theseus, Hermia, Bottom, and the rest. I would not, however, go so far as Harold C. Goddard, who speaks of the fairies as unequivocally representing "a vaster unseen world by which the actions of men are affected and overruled." Shakespeare's art is surely not so blatantly allegorical. It is not so much the fairies per se as the *mystery* of the fairies—the very aura of evanescence and ambiguity surrounding their life on stage—that points to a mysteriousness in our own existence, and specifically in such ambivalent earthly matters as love, luck, imagination, and even faith. These are the elements of human experience with which the fairies are again and again associated. As Shakespeare plays his sly games with the insubstantial fairies, we are forced by the ambivalence in their status to ask questions, ultimately unanswerable, about the substance of those mortal experiences with which they are linked.

This suggestiveness can best be illustrated by looking at the crucial exchange between Theseus and Hippolyta about the experiences of the lovers in the forest, a *locus classicus* for every study reading the play in terms of the themes of illusion, art, or the creative imagination. Certainly Theseus touches these issues when he cautions against the fantasies created by the seething brains of the lunatic, the lover, and the poet:

> Such tricks hath strong imagination,
> That, if it would but apprehend some joy,
> It comprehends some bringer of that joy;
> Or in the night, imagining some fear,
> How easy is a bush suppos'd a bear!   (V. i. 18–22)

By such explanation this advocate of daytime reason wishes to dismiss the reports of strange events in the midsummer night. Hippolyta objects by raising a question that asks more than merely whether fairies can truly be found wandering in the woods nearby:

> But all the story of the night told over,
> And all their minds transfigur'd so together,
> More witnesseth than fancy's images,
> And grows to something of great constancy;
> Yet howsoever, strange and admirable.   (V. i. 23–27)

Naturally, upon hearing this we comfortably assure ourselves of the secret presence of the fairies, and, if we are alert, we may also enjoy the fine irony that those fairies—and Theseus, too, and his speech—are all products of the seething brain of a poet. But this does not really exhaust the suggestiveness of the exchange. Behind Hippolyta's observation lies the question whether the "olde daunce" of love so brilliantly represented by the round in the nighttime woods does not reveal something orderly and purposeful behind its apparent chaos. The fairies are (among other things) the metamorphic agency of love personified, pansy-juice and all; and an ambivalence in the status of the fairies implies an ambivalence in the status of love. In the language of Theseus' rationalistic analysis, love is an apprehended joy and the fairies are the comprehended bringers of that joy. That defines the fairies' function fairly well, but literary symbols are not so easily separated from the realities to which they point. If the fairies are complete delusions, then love itself will seem a delusion; if the fairies are real, then love, however incomprehensible to daytime reason, will seem something of great constancy, substantial, strange, and maybe even admirable. Shakespeare's puzzle goes beyond the puzzles of art: the greatest mystery is not that of the fairies but of life.

—Ronald E. Miller, "*A Midsummer Night's Dream:* The Fairies, Bottom, and the Mystery of Things," *Shakespeare Quarterly* 26, No. 3 (Summer 1975): 254–56

J. WALTER HERBERT ON THEOLOGY IN *A MIDSUMMER NIGHT'S DREAM*

[J. Walter Herbert (b. 1938), a professor of English at Southwestern University, is the author of *Dearest Beloved: The Hawthornes and the Making of the Middle-Class Family* (1993). In this extract from *Oberon's Mazéd World* (1977), Herbert examines the theology of *A Midsummer Night's Dream.*]

Three characters in *A Midsummer Night's Dream* assured play-goers in 1595, as they assure you now, that Athens, Babylon, and all they contain are not worth inquiry, inductive or other. Bottom, remembering wonderful events in the Athenian wood, says, "Man is but an Asse, if hee goe about expound this dreame." Hippolyta finds the mechanicals' interlude "the silliest stuffe, that ever I heard." Robin Goodfellow belittles the whole play: "this weake and idle theame, / No more yielding but a dreame." Those who chose to do so heard in Bottom, Hippolyta, and Robin the voice of authority soberly prescribing a passive response to the comedy. Most relaxing! But though the *Dream* has power to enchant children and sheriffs, many of us, willing to call the Puck a liar, allowed our minds exercise upon themes not altogether weak.

We who liked to ask large questions and seek answers by the inductive route felt a special invitation. As I said earlier, inductive thought seems to me a highly individual process. I confess I had, like Hamlet, combination of naturalist aspirations and religious conscience. In this last chapter I shall first recapitulate my theologically biased initial responses and then acknowledge a sequence at the end of which laughter had dissolved my worries.

I did not need much discernment to recognize that, in an Athens containing Oberon, Titania, Robin, and the fairies, spirits influence events. The notion that I might be witnessing a cosmic comedy began to dawn on me when I heard Titania bemoan the misplaced seasons and the excessive rain. Noah and Aeneas, I remembered, endured falling weather precipitated by divine anger. I said to myself, "But the play has not shown a drop of water. Hermia has complained of a 'want of raine.' The plans laid by Theseus, Hippolyta, Lysander, Hermia, and Quince's whole crew of actors imply good days and nights out of doors. Why Titania's dismal weather report?" In my answer I recognized that I was imitating the form of Lysander's argument that the course of true love does not run smooth. "By Jove," I said to myself, "people are making the heavy weather that counts. Egeus' tyranny over his daughter, Theseus' harsh legalism, Demetrius' fickleness, Helena's treachery—such behavior, out of kilter and out of character, reflects Oberon's disordered household. Surely we'll see more oddities."

A few minutes later I saw Demetrius come in, Helena hot after him, and heard her disgusted comment:

> Apollo flies and Daphne holds the chase:
> The Dove pursues the Griffon: the milde Hinde
> Makes speede to catch the Tigre. Bootelesse speede,
> When cowardise pursues, and valour flies.

I hardly knew which delighted me more, the comedy or my own brilliant prediction.

"Yet the deities' quarrel," I later mused, "has to be coupled with their other actions in a single community of occasions." I noticed that Oberon and Titania meddle directly with things on the Athenian earth. Titania supervises the welfare of flowers. Oberon takes sides with Helena. Both are bent on making

Theseus' and Hippolyta's wedding happy. Joys as well as griefs and insanities in Athens perhaps depend on Oberon's and Titania's passions.

I heard a pun in Robin's "What fooles these mortals bee!" Robin was talking about young lovers, but his words fit the artisans too, and even Theseus. The mortals' crazy behavior shows them fools in the commonest sense. I also took *fools* to mean helpless puppets, as in Romeo's anguished "O I am fortune's fool!" (*Romeo and Juliet,* III, i, 141) Robin, I thought, speaks with bad grace. He himself is a tool of the same natural force that has afflicted the mortals with midsummer madness.

Remembering my wonder how far men are to blame for acts of God in my English world, I reflected that a *Dream* theology must belittle human responsibility. Athenian mortals' wickedness, like troubles and joys, spins off from fairy discord. So when Oberon and Titania at length agree and Athenians grow virtuous as well as happy, I chuckled, "O my prophetic soul!"

I became aware of questions corresponding to questions in basic theology, the first of which involves nature's reliability, a necessary postulate for all experimental investigators. Not a few Elizabethan Christians believed that good deeds help a fellow thrive on earth and reach heaven. But others, especially Calvinists, argued that God is not subject to persuasion, that human righteousness is but filthy rags, futile attempts to bribe God. Good things come to the just and the unjust, and so do bad things. I observed that mischievous Robin perpetrates mischief on Bottom and his friends simply because he notices an opportunity. Bottom does nothing to deserve translation. The lovers do nothing to earn help. Athens mimics Calvinists' grace and election, I decided, but mimics it gaily and indeed sympathetically, without venom.

Whereas in Calvin's world, under an omniscient, omnipotent God, the interesting question about trouble concerns God's benevolence, in Lysander's world the interesting question concerns Oberon's knowledge and power. Though Oberon knows more than men, and lays plans, he learns about an event only after it has happened. Though more powerful than men, he is not all-powerful. He obeys the cycle of day and night. He con-

trols Titania, Robin, and men by perseverance and resourceful-
ness rather than by absolute authority. When he takes an interest, however, Oberon can bring a mortal's plan to a better
fruition than the mortal intended.

—J. Walter Herbert, *Oberon's Mazéd World* (Baton Rouge:
Louisiana State University Press, 1977), pp. 153–55

WILLIAM EMPSON ON COMEDY IN *A MIDSUMMER NIGHT'S DREAM*

[William Empson (1906–1984) was one of the most
distinguished British critics of the twentieth century.
Among his works are *Seven Types of Ambiguity* (1930)
and *Some Versions of Pastoral* (1935). In this extract
from his posthumously collected *Essays on Shakespeare*
(1986), Empson compares the comical elements in *A
Midsummer Night's Dream* to the madcap world of
P. G. Wodehouse.]

When Oberon remarks that he and the lovers will remember
the night as "but the fierce vexation of a dream", he is not giving an order, and some fierce dreams do get remembered long
and vividly (or at least you can remember your reconstruction
of them). The real feeling of Brooks, I submit, is: thank God we
don't have to watch a lady actually giving herself to a stinking
hairy worker. "Even a controlled suggestion of carnal bestiality
is surely impossible", he remarks.

These cloudy but provocative phrases conceal a struggle
which had better have been brought into the open. The opponent is Jan Kott, who wrote *Shakespeare Our Contemporary*
(1964), and the Peter Brook production (1970) which drama-
tised his findings. I take my stand beside the other old buffers
here. Kott is ridiculously indifferent to the letter of the play and
labours to befoul its spirit. And yet the Victorian attitude to it
also feels oppressively false, and has a widespread influence.

We need here to consider Madeline Bassett, who figures decisively in the plot of a number of stories by P. G. Wodehouse. This unfortunate girl, though rich, young, handsome and tolerably good-tempered, has a habit of saying, for example, that a dear little baby is born every time a wee fairy blows its nose. She never repeats herself but keeps steadily within this range. It excites nausea and horror in almost all the young men who have become entangled with her, and their only hope of escape without rudeness is to marry her to the sub-human Augustus Fink-Nottle. Such is the mainspring for a series of farces. However remotely, her fancies are clearly derived from Shakespeare's *Dream,* and Wodehouse was a very understanding, well-read man, with a thorough grasp of this general revulsion. Such is the strength of our opponents. It is no use for the present editor to complain in a footnote that the Brook production lacked "charm": a too-determined pursuit of charm was what spelt doom for poor Madeline Bassett.

What a production needs to do is to make clear that Oberon and Titania are global powers, impressive when in action. There is nothing to grumble about in the tenderness of the fairy scenes towards small wild flowers and young children, but it needs balancing. Many thinkers, summarised by Cornelius Agrippa, had believed in these Spirits of Nature, neither angels nor devils, in the first part of the sixteenth century, but Luther and Calvin denounced the belief, and the Counter-Reformation largely agreed, so further discussion in print was prevented by censorship. But ten of the Cambridge colleges, at the time of the play, had Agrippa's treatise in their libraries. So the dons were not hiding it from the children, and it gives you positively encouraging advice about how to raise nymphs from watermeadows. The New Astronomy was in the same position: learned books arguing in its favour could not get a licence, though a mere expression of agreement with it was not penalised. And Copernicus in his Introduction had actually claimed support from Hermes Trismegistus, who was considered the ancient source of the belief in Middle Spirits.

The fairy scenes here say a good deal about astronomy, though none of it further out than the Moon; and there are other reasons for thinking that the public had largely accepted the daily rotation of the Earth, but thought its yearly orbit to be supported by obscure arguments and probably dangerous.

If these spirits control Nature over the whole globe, they need to move about it at a tolerable speed. When the audience is first confronted by the magic wood, at the start of Act II a fairy tells Puck, "I am going everywhere, faster than the moon's sphere", because she has been given the job of putting the smell into the cowslips. As they all come out at about the same time, this requires enormously rapid movement, continually changing in direction. She should be found panting against a tree-trunk, having a short rest at human size, but when in action her body must be like a bullet. It seems tiresome to have human-sized spirits described as very tiny, but it is standard doctrine that they could make themselves so, and we find that they could also make themselves very heavy. It is an old textual crux that Puck speaks to Oberon of "our stamp", but immediately after this warning we see him do their magic stamp, which should be echoed tersely by a deep-voiced drum under the stage. Thus we are prepared for Oberon and Titania to "shake the ground" when they dance good fortune to the lovers: the drums now become a form of music, echoing each step (there is a very faint repetition of it when they are dancing off-stage in the palace bedroom). Then, immediately after shaking the ground, they go up on the crane, apparently weightless. Oberon remarks:

> We the globe can compass soon,
> Swifter than the wandering moon.

He is thus recalling what the fairy said at the start. He does not say they will do it now, only that they can do what is needed with a comfortable margin, if they are to dance again in the palace soon after midnight.

—William Empson, "Fairy Flight in *A Midsummer Night's Dream*" (1979), *Essays on Shakespeare* (Cambridge: Cambridge University Press, 1986), pp. 223–25

J. DENNIS HUSTON ON PARODY IN *A MIDSUMMER NIGHT'S DREAM*

[J. Dennis Huston is coeditor of *Classics of the Renaissance Theater: Seven English Plays* (1969) and the author of *Shakespeare's Comedies of Play* (1981), from which the following extract is taken. Here, Huston examines the use of parody in *A Midsummer Night's Dream,* whereby Shakespeare deliberately reveals to his audience that they are only watching a play.]

⟨. . .⟩ *A Midsummer Night's Dream* is a play notable almost as much for its parodies as for its other, more obvious metamorphoses. In addition to Bottom's deflation of Petruchio, the play also offers us: a dramatic travesty of the tragic love story of Pyramus and Thisbe, which doubles as a reductive version of the lovers' mistakings in the wood, and may even triple as a comic rendering of Shakespeare's own dramatic presentation of the story of Romeo and Juliet (if composed by then); a parody of the relationship between the surrogate playwright figure of Oberon and his incorrigible servant-actor Puck in the alliance between the inept playwright Quince and his uncontrollable principal player Bottom; a ridiculous reversal of the fairy tale situation of the princess held in bondage by the monster, in the fairy queen's rapturous capture of the ass-headed Bottom; and Bottom's ludicrously garbled version of a part of St Paul's Epistle to the Corinthians, in his soliloquy upon awaking from charmed sleep. What these parodies signal is the extent to which Shakespeare is mentally playing with the art of playwriting in this work, for a parody is a kind of intellectual play, which calls attention to the mastery of a particular constricting form by comically reshaping that form to new purposes. In order to understand how Shakespeare plays with the limitations of dramatic form in *A Midsummer Night's Dream,* it is thus necessary to see how he uses parody in that world. And since Bottom is the principal instrument of parody—and also an important indicator of meaning—in this play, he can serve as a point of departure for this discussion.

I begin near the end, with the fourth act and Bottom the player alone on a stage, with drama reduced to its elemental two boards and a passion. Only here, for a moment, there is not even any passion, for the player is asleep, transported beyond the boundaries of the waking world by a magical charm. It is a charm of some considerable range and magnitude since Bottom is not the only one to have been affected by it: earlier it has struck 'more dead / Than common sleep' (IV. i. 84–5) the senses of four Athenian lovers, and long before that it has partly enthralled the faculties of the audience. So now, although they do not sleep like Bottom, they have been transported out of the ordinary and into a world elsewhere. In such a world strange and extraordinary effects are played on their senses, without even attracting notice as strange and extraordinary. There a tedious brief play some ten words long wears away the three hours between supper and bedtime; there the moon, new for Theseus' wedding, has already waxed to brightness by the time of the rustics' production that same night; and there Bottom may lie asleep in plain view of the audience without really being seen.

He has not even, like Oberon earlier, had to *ask* for a willing suspension of disbelief by announcing himself invisible. The lovers and Theseus have just played a scene all around him, and their obliviousness to his presence has conditioned the audience not to see him either. Thus when the lovers exit towards the temple, the audience confronts an empty stage. Only when Bottom fills that emptiness by stirring to life does he make the members of the audience similarly awaken from the binding spell Shakespeare has woven over them. In their theater seats many of them, like Bottom on the stage, will stir in surprise at what has just happened to them, as momentarily the playwright makes them aware of his art *as* art.

This particular example of a Shakespearean *Verfremdungseffekt* does not, however, end quite here; instead it edges over into the beginning of Bottom's soliloquy. He begins: 'When my cue comes . . .' (IV. i. 204) and the audience may briefly share with the actor playing Bottom the very real knowledge that his cue has indeed come. By then, however, Bottom has already regained his footing literally and dramatically; and in his attempt to summon up first a company of lost players and then a remembrance of things past, he again magically carries the audience away from itself and into a 'most rare vision' (IV. i. 208).

Here briefly the themes and actions of the play are focused in a moment of dramatic concentration, whose importance is emphasized in a number of different ways. First, the alienation effect which accompanies Bottom's awakening, by temporarily interrupting the audience's emotional involvement in the play, encourages intellectual speculation about the meaning of the work. Second, the very episode itself is a conspicuous reflection of the action which has just preceded it, when the four sleeping lovers are found by Theseus and his party. Like Bottom, they all awake from the spell of Oberon's magic to contemplate a dream vision in which they have experienced a kind of metamorphosis and a disorienting love affair.

—J. Dennis Huston, *Shakespeare's Comedies of Play* (New York: Columbia University Press, 1981), pp. 97–99

ROGER WARREN ON TITANIA, OBERON, AND PUCK

[Roger Warren is the author of *Staging Shakespeare's Late Plays* (1990). In this extract from his study of *A Midsummer Night's Dream,* Warren comments on Shakespeare's use of fairies in the play.]

In their opening quarrel, Shakespeare makes Oberon and Titania immediately striking characters by giving them human passions; but he also needs to differentiate them from human beings, without losing that sense of tangible reality. As Peter Hall puts it, 'fairy tales must be concrete if they are to be human and not whimsical' (*Sunday Times,* 26 Jan. 1969). Shakespeare achieves this by presenting them in terms of the natural world in which they live, evoked in concrete detail: the loveliest, most delicate wild flowers, the sunrise over the sea— and also frost, rain, and mud. Shakespeare varies the image he presents of the countryside in order to reflect different aspects of the fairies themselves. This can be demonstrated by considering four passages in detail, first Titania's account of the chaotic weather which has resulted from her quarrel with Oberon [II i 81–117], and then three of Oberon's major speeches: his description of Titania's bower [II i 249–56], his evocation of the sunrise [III ii 388–93], and his vision which introduces the magic flower [II i 148–68]. Each of these passages is placed at a dramatically important moment in the play. Each helps to characterise the fairies and their world, and to establish what kind of spirits they are. ⟨. . .⟩

The fairies of *A Midsummer Night's Dream* are not like this at all. Titania did not steal the changeling boy from his mortal mother; on the contrary, she loves and cherishes him for his mother's sake, even at the cost of a violent quarrel with Oberon. While, of course, the indirect result of this quarrel is unfortunate for the mortals because it inflicts a wretched summer upon them, the fairies' direct dealings with the mortals are benevolent. Although something of the traditional dangerous fairies survives in Puck's enjoyment of misleading the mechanicals and the lovers ('this their jangling I esteem a sport' [III ii 353]), even he is mischievous rather than malevolent: 'those things do best please me / That befall preposterously' [III ii 120–1]. And however mixed Puck's motives may be, Oberon's reason for intervening in the affairs of the lovers is sympathetic and entirely benevolent:

> Fare thee well, nymph. Ere he do leave this grove
> Thou shalt fly him, and he shall seek thy love.   [II i 245–6]

In making Oberon and Titania essentially benevolent towards mortals, Shakespeare was significantly modifying a tradition which he accepted in other plays.

Whereas Titania's speech about the bad weather expresses the disastrous consequences of the fairies' quarrel by creating a vivid picture of the unpleasant features of the natural world, three important speeches by Oberon evoke the wholesome and desirable beauty of the countryside to suggest the fairies' positive aspects and the source of their power. A very clear example is Oberon's description of Titania's bower,

> a bank where the wild thyme blows,
> Where oxlips and the nodding violet grows,
> Quite overcanopied with luscious woodbine,
> With sweet muskroses and with eglantine.   [II i 249–52]

This speech is more than a piece of verbal scene-painting. The bank seems to take on a life of its own. The language insists on the positive qualities of the natural world. In particular, the adjectives are carefully chosen to suggest delicacy ('*nodding* violet'), richness ('*luscious* woodbine') and attractiveness ('*sweet* muskroses'). The wild thyme 'blows' fragrance into the air; 'quite overcanopied' suggests a sense of security for Titania as she sleeps. The dramatic effect of the passage as a whole is to associate Titania herself with the positive beauty of her surroundings.

> —Roger Warren, *A Midsummer Night's Dream* (London: Macmillan Press, 1983), pp. 13–14, 17–18

NORTHROP FRYE ON PUCK AND THE CREATURES OF THE WOOD-WORLD

[Northrop Frye (1912–1991), formerly a professor of English at Victoria University in Toronto, was a highly respected literary critic. Among his works are *Anatomy of Criticism* (1957), *A Natural Perspective: The Development of Shakespearean Comedy and Romance* (1965), and *Fools of Time* (1967), a study of Shakespeare's tragedies. In this extract (taken from a volume of his university lectures on Shakespeare), Frye investigates the darker nature of Puck.]

Pucks were a category of spirits who were often sinister, and the Puck of this play is clearly mischievous. But we are expressly told by Oberon that the fairies of whom he's the king are "spirits of another sort," not evil and not restricted to darkness.

So the title of the play simply emphasizes the difference between the two worlds of the action, the waking world of Theseus's court and the fairy world of Oberon. Let's go back to the three parts of the comic action: the opening situation hostile to true love, the middle part of dissolving identities, and the final resolution. The first part contains a threat of possible death to Hermia. Similar threats are found in other Shake-speare comedies: in *The Comedy of Errors* a death sentence hangs over a central character until nearly the end of the play. This comic structure fits inside a pattern of death, disappearance and return that's far wider in scope than theatrical comedy. We find it even in the central story of Christianity, with its Friday of death, Saturday of disappearance and Sunday of return. Scholars who have studied this pattern in religion, mythology and legend think it derives from observing the moon waning, then disappearing, then reappearing as a new moon.

At the opening Theseus and Hippolyta have agreed to hold their wedding at the next new moon, now four days off. They speak of four days, although the rhetorical structure runs in threes: Hippolyta is wooed, won and wed "With pomp, with triumph and with revelling." (This reading depends also on a reasonable, if not certain, emendation: "new" for "now" in the tenth line.) Theseus compares his impatience to the comedy situation of a young man waiting for someone older to die and leave him money. The Quince company discover from an almanac that there will be moonshine on the night that they will be performing, but apparently there is not enough, and so they introduce a character called Moonshine. His appearance touches off a very curious reprise of the opening dialogue. Hippolyta says "I am aweary of this moon: would he would change!", and Theseus answers that he seems to be on the wane, "but yet, in courtesy . . . we must stay the time." It's as though this ghastly play contains in miniature, and caricature, the themes of separation, postponement, and confusions of reality and fantasy that have organized the play surrounding it.

According to the indications in the text, the night in the wood should be a moonless night, but in fact there are so many references to the moon that it seems to be still there, even though obscured by clouds. It seems that this wood is a fairyland with its own laws of time and space, a world where Oberon has just blown in from India and where Puck can put a girdle round the earth in forty minutes. So it's not hard to accept such a world as an antipodal one, like the world of dreams itself, which, although we make it fit into our waking-time schedules, still keeps to its own quite different rhythms. A curious image of Hermia's involving the moon has echoes of this; she's protesting that she will never believe Lysander unfaithful:

> I'll believe as soon
> This whole earth may be bored, and that the moon
> May through the centre creep, and so displease
> Her brother's noontide with th'Antipodes.   (III.ii. 52–55)

A modern reader might think of the opening of "The Walrus and the Carpenter." The moon, in any case, seems to have a good deal to do with both worlds. In the opening scene Lysander speaks of Demetrius as "this spotted and inconstant man," using two common epithets for the moon, and in the last act Theseus speaks of "the lunatic, the lover and the poet," where "lunatic" has its full Elizabethan force of "moonstruck."

The inhabitants of the wood-world are the creatures of legend and folk tale and mythology and abandoned belief. Theseus regards them as projections of the human imagination, and as having a purely subjective existence. The trouble is that we don't know the extent of our own minds, or what's in that mental world that we half create and half perceive, in Wordsworth's phrase. The tiny fairies that wait on Bottom— Mustardseed and Peaseblossom and the rest—come from Celtic fairy lore, as does the Queen Mab of Mercutio's speech, who also had tiny fairies in her train. Robin Goodfellow is more Anglo-Saxon and Teutonic. His propitiatory name, "Goodfellow," indicates that he could be dangerous, and his fairy friend says that one of his amusements is to "Mislead night-wanderers, laughing at their harm." A famous book a little later than Shakespeare, Robert Burton's *Anatomy of Melancholy,* mentions fire spirits who mislead travellers with illusions, and says "We commonly call them pucks." The fairy world clearly would not do as a democracy: there has to be a king in charge like Oberon, who will see that Puck's rather primitive sense of humour doesn't get too far out of line.

—Northrop Frye, *"A Midsummer Night's Dream," Northrop Frye on Shakespeare,* ed. Robert Soudler (New Haven: Yale University Press, 1986), pp. 43–45

[David Richman (b. 1951), a professor of theater at the University of New Hampshire, is the author of *Laughter, Pain, and Wonder: Shakespeare's Comedies and the Audience in the Theatre* (1990), from which the following extract is taken. Here, Richman argues that *A Midsummer Night's Dream* successfully weaves wonder into comedy.]

The attempts to weave wonder into comedy reach their first complete success in *A Midsummer Night's Dream*. The play is remarkable for many qualities, not the least of which is verse that gives full expression to the marvels the dramatist represents. The king and queen of fairyland astonish the spectators with their language as well as their power. Titania's attendants and even Puck are creatures of a different order from the contending sovereigns of fairyland, and the difference should be made clear in production. In Shakespeare's time Oberon was played by an adult actor, Titania by the star boy, and the other fairies by children of lesser abilities. In a 1978 R.S.C. production the attendant fairies were puppets, and in Peter Brook's famous production, as well as in several others not so well known, all the fairies, including Oberon, became trapeze artists.

The manner in which the fairies' verse contrasts with the verse of their king and queen suggests differences of degree and kind. The fairies and Puck characteristically speak in tetrameter or pentameter couplets. They exult in and exalt the diminutive. Their verse is full of dewdrops, cowslips, long-legged spinners, and hedgehogs. The mischiefs in which Puck delights are typically farcical pranks—tempting lusty horses, humiliating old ladies, or spoiling the beer. Oberon and Titania speak mostly in blank verse that grows ever more majestic. In describing and enacting their continuing quarrel, the king and queen make clear that their discord is reflected in all sublunary nature. Shakespeare is here varying a rhetorical device that he uses throughout his career. But Titania and Oberon are not mortals like Romeo or Richard II, who imagine all nature to be participating in their grief and rage. Rather these are the very spirits of nature, the originals of natural turbulence. What they describe is not an imagined but an actual result of their anger.

To express this turbulence, the playwright gives Oberon and Titania verse that employs striking rhythmic and figurative resources. The ear encounters inverted iambs and spondees, which force strongly stressed syllables into direct alignment with each other. There is also frequent enjambment and a flexible use of the caesura, which occurs often in the middle of a foot and occasionally in the middle of an inverted foot. The rhythm of a line like "Fall in the fresh lap of the crimson rose" has a twofold effect: the juxtaposition of strongly stressed syllables forces the speaker to retard; accented syllables and the caesura, all occurring in surprising places, create an impression of emotional agitation. Moreover, the prosopopoeia and antonomasia in these speeches invest the unseasonal prodigies with human passion and torment:

> The human mortals want their winter here;
> No night is now with hymn or carol blest;
> Therefore the moon, the governess of floods,
> Pale in her anger, washes all the air,
> That rheumatic diseases do abound.
> And thorough this distemperature we see
> The seasons alter: hoary-headed frosts
> Fall in the fresh lap of the crimson rose;
> And on old Hiems' thin and icy crown
> An odorous chaplet of sweet summer buds
> Is, as in mockery, set. The spring, the summer,
> The childing autumn, angry winter, change
> Their wonted liveries; and the mazed world,
> By their increase, now knows not which is which.
> And this same progeny of evils comes
> From our debate, from our dissension;
> We are their parents and original.   (2.1.101–17)

A key to Titania's speech can be found in a word near its end that Shakespeare typically charges with many meanings. The fairy queen speaks of "the mazed world," calling to mind her earlier reference to "the quaint mazes in the wanton green" (2.1.99). The world in its confusion has become literally and figuratively a maze, a labyrinth in which no right path can be found. But the word takes on also its second sense of "amazed," that is, astonished, struck with wonder by the alterations. The speech in performance will stand or fall on the actress's ability to convince the audience of her character's astonishment and shame that she and Oberon are damaging the natural world. To be sure, they are engaged in a farcical love-brawl, but love that is capable of such effects is a great and terrible passion that evokes a Sidneyan admiration. The rage and power of Oberon and Titania stir potentially tragic responses. Peter Brook's recognition and manipulation of these responses may constitute his famous production's greatest achievements.

No Shakespearean comedy offers wider scope to the imagination of directors, designers, and actors, and in no Shakespearean comedy is it more necessary to observe Bruno Walter's admonition to select from among the limitless imaginative possibilities those essential to the play as a whole. Although many of the play's scenes require spectacular visual display and startling or hilarious stage business, the second-act quarrel between Oberon and Titania must guide the audience to focus on language and passion. The director's principal responsibility in this scene is to find actors who possess the talent to speak verse with beauty and power. Having found and worked with such actors, the director must insure that the scenery, lighting, and costumes aid the spectators' response without competing for their attention.

—David Richman, *Laughter, Pain, and Wonder: Shakespeare's Comedies and the Audience in the Theatre* (Newark: University of Delaware Press, 1990), pp. 97–99

JAMES L. CALDERWOOD ON THE RELATIONSHIP BETWEEN PLAYERS AND AUDIENCE IN *A MIDSUMMER NIGHT'S DREAM*

[James L. Calderwood is a noted Shakespearean scholar and the author of *To Be or Not to Be: Negation and Metadrama in* Hamlet (1983) and *Shakespeare and the Denial of Death* (1987). In this extract from his study of *A Midsummer Night's Dream*, Calderwood studies the relationship between the characters of the play and the audience.]

⟨. . .⟩ before we theatregoers can retire, Puck comes forth to ask what we, who have o'erseen all, have actually seen. Like Bottom gearing up to play Pyramus, Puck says in effect, 'Let the audience look to their eyes' (I.ii.22), and if we cannot do that for ourselves, he will do it for us. In fact, he will look to our eyes in a couple of senses. First, he will look *into* our eyes. As a representative of the play, he is anxious, as players always are, to be the desire of the other, to be as his audience would have him; so he looks into our mirroring eyes to discover what that might be. What he hopes to see there is not of course a dismissive Sartrian look of the sort implied by Theseus' line 'the best in this kind are but shadows' (V.i.210) but something more auspiciously Lacanian, perhaps the lost loving gaze of the mother that most actors would like to recapture.

But ⟨. . .⟩ the gaze in which players can be caught and their play defined is itself vulnerable to entrapment, most noticeably when it encounters anamorphic diversions. Thus the audience to whose judgement Puck so humbly defers should beware being taken in, for in looking to our eyes the sly one looks not only inquiringly *into* them but also therapeutically *to* them, tending to our gaze as he tended to that of Lysander and Demetrius. Some of the flower juice he drops in our eyes is contained in his invitation to 'think but this', that all 'these visions' have come dreamingly from within ourselves and hence cannot be attributed, if we do not like them, to a bad play or a clumsy performance. He seems to have taken his cue from the Prologue to Lyly's *Sapho and Phao* (1584), who, with Elizabeth in attendance, makes amends beforehand: 'We all, and I on knee for all, entreat that your Highness imagine yourself to be in a deep dream, that staying the conclusion, in your rising, your Majesty vouchsafe but to say *And so you waked.*' This is but minimally apologetic, for to be in a 'deep dream' is not necessarily a bad thing, nor is a play that puts one there. Puck speaks more disparagingly of a theme 'weak and idle' and un-'yielding' as a dream, as if he were of Mercutio's mind, who debunked dreams as 'begot of nothing but vain fantasy' (*Romeo and Juliet,* I.iv.98). This view of things may exonerate the players, but at the expense of making their performance dissolve into airy nothing. That, according to William Hazlitt, leaving a rather operatic performance of the play at Covent Garden in 1816, is precisely what it ought to do. For, as he complained in an influential report in *The Examiner,* plays like *A Midsummer Night's Dream* are flagrantly inhospitable to the romantic imagination:

> Poetry and the stage do not agree together. The attempt to reconcile them fails not only of effect, but of decorum. The *ideal* can have no place upon the stage, which is a picture without perspective; everything there is in the foreground. That which is merely an airy shape, a dream, a passing thought, immediately becomes an unmanageable reality. Where all is left to the imagination, every circumstance has an equal chance of being kept in mind, and tells according to the mixed impression of all that has been suggested. But the imagination cannot sufficiently qualify the impression of the senses. Any offence given to the eye is not to be got rid of by explanation. Thus Bottom's head in the play [as imagined while reading] is a fantastic illusion, produced by magic spells: on the stage it is an ass's head, and nothing more; certainly a very strange costume for a gentleman to appear in. Fancy cannot be represented any more than a simile can be painted; and it is as idle to attempt it as to personate Wall or Moonshine. Fairies are not incredible, but fairies six feet high are so. (*The Examiner,* January 1816)

Even more loudly than *Henry V,* then, *A Midsummer Night's Dream* seems to call for a choral prologue which would apologise for 'the flat unraised spirits that hath dared / On this unworthy scaffold to bring forth / So great an object'—or, rather, so small an object—as fairies. Shakespeare does indeed apologise in Puck's Epilogue, asking us to forgive all offences and to imagine that what Hazlitt would prefer to happen has happened: actors, stage, the theatre itself have all vanished, and we who thought we were an audience have awakened to find ourselves, strangely enough, in a theatre, rubbing our eyes and wondering like Keats, 'Was it a vision, or a waking dream?'

Since waking and wondering are precisely what six of the characters in *A Midsummer Night's Dream* spend much of their time doing, we may wonder just whom we should take for a model. Should we wake like Lysander and Demetrius, eyes beflowered and affections gone mad, or like all the lovers later, affections set right but memories confused, or, worst of all, like Bottom, mind and senses bafflingly unhinged? No doubt some of the audience will be as anxious as Demetrius to put fairies and fantasy behind them—'These things seem small and undistinguishable, / Like far-off mountains turned into clouds' (IV.i.186–7). But surely there will be others, less certain, who will murmur with Hermia 'Methinks I see [this play] with parted eye, / When everything seems double' (188–9), and still others who, like Bottom and Samuel Pepys, will have seen everything and experienced nothing. Who does Puck have in mind for us?

—James L. Calderwood, *A Midsummer Night's Dream* (New York: Twayne, 1992), pp. 147–49

DAVID WILES ON SEXUALITY IN *A MIDSUMMER NIGHT'S DREAM*

[David Wiles, a professor of drama and theater studies at Royal Holloway College, University of London, has written *The Early Plays of Robin Hood* (1981), *Shakespeare's Clowns: Actor and Text in the Elizabethan Playhouse* (1987), and *The Masks of Menander: Sign and Meaning in Greek and Roman Performance* (1991). In this extract from his study of *A Midsummer Night's Dream,* Wiles examines the comic sexual encounter between Bottom and Titania, which he sees as a wry reflection and parody of actual Elizabethan marriage practices.]

The encounter between Bottom and Titania is a parodic inversion. A real bride should be modest, not sexually voracious, a virgin and not sexually experienced. The real groom should display more sexual enthusiasm, yet not surrender to animal instinct. Jonson is clear about the man's duty:

> Tonight is Venus' vigil kept.
> This night no bridegroom ever slept;
> And if the fair bride do,
> The married say 'tis his fault too.

Bottom's failure to stay awake is conceived as the ultimate form of inappropriate behaviour in a nuptial context. In the context of a real wedding, we can see how the parody would have a social function of some importance. The night is to be an initiation for both parties, and is a rite of passage that has no modern equivalent. A couple who have only met each other a few times in relatively formal circumstances are suddenly going to meet naked under the sheets, with an obligation to give a good account of themselves the next morning. ⟨. . .⟩

Once the sexual act has taken place in Titania's bower, Oberon is able to obtain from Titania that which he most wants, the boy. Titania's withholding of the boy is the source of all the dissent in Fairyland, and the chaotic inversion of the seasons. Pregnancy is vividly and rapturously evoked, likened to the way a sail grows 'big-bellied with the wanton wind' (II.i.129). Titania is custodian of the boy, but after her consummation with Bottom, she transfers the boy to Oberon's bower. The symbolism is clear in an epithalamic context. The boy sought by Oberon parallels the male heir which all bridegrooms seek from their brides. The poets are explicit on this subject. Spenser hopes that Cynthia, who has charge of 'women's labours' may 'the chaste womb inform with timely seed'. Genius is asked to ensure that the 'timely fruit of this same night' arrives safely. Jonson calls for 'the birth, by Cynthia hasted' in the epithalamium to *Hymenaei,* and in the epithalamium after the 'Haddington Masque' he calls for a babe who will 'Wear the long honours of his father's deed'. The masculine pronoun seemed self-evident. Herrick echoes the theme, and we notice how dew is again associated with procreation:

> May the bed, and this short night,
> Know the fullness of delight!
> Pleasures, many here attend ye,
> And ere long, a boy, Love send ye,
> Curled and comely, and so trim,
> Maids (in time) may ravish him.
> Thus a dew of graces fall
> On ye both; goodnight to all.

Aristocratic marriages were undertaken in order that a family line could be continued. Brides were under enormous psychological pressure to yield up a male child. The pressure which Oberon places upon a reluctant Titania echoes that urgent social demand. The entire central action of the play is a dream-like (or nightmare) evocation of a wedding night. The Athenian scenes are associated with the public, patriarchal aspect of marriage. The young lovers have to obtain parental consent at the start of the play, and in the last act they conform to the social expectation that males will be capable of witty banter, females will be modestly silent. The woodland scenes are asso-ciated with the private, nocturnal, female-dominated aspect of marriage. The wood, closely associated with the maying cere-mony, functions as an extended May/nuptial bower. As in a nuptial, it is 'deep midnight' when the lovers escape to the secrecy of the 'bower'. Here they fall prey to Puck and other malicious spirits. The long-delayed sexual act is suggested mimetically by the dance when Oberon and Titania hold hands and 'rock the ground whereon these sleepers be' (IV.i.85). In the morning when the lovers are woken to the rough music of the hounds, they receive a humiliating reveille. The reveille, as we have seen, was a time when the newly-married couple had to give an account of themselves, and satisfy interrogators that intercourse had taken place. As in the dream, so in reality a hunting song was often used to awaken the newly-weds. What the lovers in the play have learned from their experience is not clear, but in the extra-theatrical world of the audience, an actual bridal couple may well have done their share of learning and adjusting. It was not only the Queen who found the conflict between Venus and Diana very hard to reconcile. Every young bride was expected on her wedding night to put aside the cult of chastity and in an instant become a votary of Venus.

—David Wiles, *Shakespeare's Almanac: A Midsummer Night's Dream, Marriage and the Elizabethan Calendar* (Cambridge: D. S. Brewer, 1993), pp. 122–25

Works by
William Shakespeare

Venus and Adonis. 1593.

The Rape of Lucrece. 1594.

Henry VI. 1594.

Titus Andronicus. 1594.

The Taming of the Shrew. 1594.

Romeo and Juliet. 1597.

Richard III. 1597.

Richard II. 1597.

Love's Labour's Lost. 1598.

Henry IV. 1598.

The Passionate Pilgrim. 1599.

A Midsummer Night's Dream. 1600.

The Merchant of Venice. 1600.

Much Ado about Nothing. 1600.

Henry V. 1600.

The Phoenix and the Turtle. 1601.

The Merry Wives of Windsor. 1602.

Hamlet. 1603.

King Lear. 1608.

Troilus and Cressida. 1609.

Sonnets. 1609.

Pericles. 1609.

Othello. 1622.

Mr. William Shakespeares Comedies, Histories & Tragedies. Ed. John Heminge and Henry Condell. 1623 (First Folio), 1632 (Second Folio), 1663 (Third Folio), 1685 (Fourth Folio).

Poems. 1640.

Works. Ed. Nicholas Rowe. 1709. 6 vols.

Works. Ed. Alexander Pope. 1723–25. 6 vols.

Works. Ed. Lewis Theobald. 1733. 7 vols.

Works. Ed. Thomas Hanmer. 1743–44. 6 vols.

Works. Ed. William Warburton. 1747. 8 vols.

Plays. Ed. Samuel Johnson. 1765. 8 vols.

Plays and Poems. Ed. Edmond Malone. 1790. 10 vols.

The Family Shakespeare. Ed. Thomas Bowdler. 1807. 4 vols.

Works. Ed. J. Payne Collier. 1842–44. 8 vols.

Works. Ed. H. N. Hudson. 1851–56. 11 vols.

Works. Ed. Alexander Dyce. 1857. 6 vols.

Works. Ed. Richard Grant White. 1857–66. 12 vols.

Works (Cambridge Edition). Ed. William George Clark, John Glover, and William Aldis Wright. 1863–66. 9 vols.

A New Variorum Edition of the Works of Shakespeare. Ed. H. H. Furness et al. 1871– .

Works. Ed. W. J. Rolfe. 1871–96. 40 vols.

The Pitt Press Shakespeare. Ed. A. W. Verity. 1890–1905. 13 vols.

The Warwick Shakespeare. 1893–1938. 13 vols.

The Temple Shakespeare. Ed. Israel Gollancz. 1894–97. 40 vols.

The Arden Shakespeare. Ed. W. J. Craig, R. H. Case et al. 1899–1924. 37 vols.

The Shakespeare Apocrypha. Ed. C. F. Tucker Brooke. 1908.

The Yale Shakespeare. Ed. Wilbur L. Cross, Tucker Brooke, and Willard Highley Durham. 1917–27. 40 vols.

The New Shakespeare (Cambridge Edition). Ed. Arthur Quiller-Couch and John Dover Wilson. 1921–62. 38 vols.

The New Temple Shakespeare. Ed. M. R. Ridley. 1934–36. 39 vols.

Works. Ed. George Lyman Kittredge. 1936.

The Penguin Shakespeare. Ed. G. B. Harrison. 1937–59. 36 vols.

The New Clarendon Shakespeare. Ed. R. E. C. Houghton. 1938– .

The Arden Shakespeare. Ed. Una Ellis-Fermor et al. 1951– .

The Complete Pelican Shakespeare. Ed. Alfred Harbage. 1969.

The Complete Signet Classic Shakespeare. Ed. Sylvan Barnet. 1972.

The Oxford Shakespeare. Ed. Stanley Wells. 1982– .

The New Cambridge Shakespeare. Ed. Philip Brockbank. 1984– .

Works about Shakespeare and *A Midsummer Night's Dream*

Allen, John A. "Bottom and Titania." *Shakespeare Quarterly* 18 (1967): 107–17.

Andreas, James R. "Remythologizing *The Knight's Tale: A Midsummer Night's Dream* and *The Two Noble Kinsmen*." *Shakespeare Yearbook* 2 (1991): 49–67.

Bellringer, Alan W. "The Act of Change in *A Midsummer Night's Dream*." *English Studies* 64 (1983): 201–17.

Berry, Ralph. "No Exit from Arden." *Modern Language Review* 66 (1971): 11–20.

Bloom, Harold, ed. *William Shakespeare's* A Midsummer Night's Dream. New York: Chelsea House, 1987.

Briggs, Katherine M. *The Anatomy of Puck: An Examination of Fairy Beliefs and Magic among Shakespeare's Contemporaries and His Immediate Successors.* London: Routledge & Kegan Paul, 1962.

Brown, Jane K. "Discordia Concors: On the Order of *A Midsummer Night's Dream*." *Modern Language Quarterly* 49 (1987): 20–41.

Calderwood, James L. "*A Midsummer Night's Dream:* Anamorphism and Theseus' Dream." *Shakespeare Quarterly* 42 (1991): 409–30.

Donaldson, E. Talbot. "The Embarrassments of Art: *The Tale of Sir Thopas*, 'Pyramus and Thisbe,' and *A Midsummer Night's Dream*." In Donaldson's *The Swan at the Well: Shakespeare Reading Chaucer.* New Haven: Yale University Press, 1985, pp. 7–29.

Dunn, Allen. "The Indian Boy's Dream Wherein Every Mother's Son Rehearses His Part: Shakespeare's *A Midsummer Night's Dream*." *Shakespeare Studies* 20 (1988): 15–32.

Foakes, F. A. *Shakespeare: The Dark Comedies to the Last Plays—From Satire to Celebration*. Charlottesville: University Press of Virginia, 1971.

Franke, Wolfgang. "The Logic of Double-Entendre in *A Midsummer Night's Dream*." *Philological Quarterly* 58 (1979): 282–97.

Garber, Marjorie B. *Dream in Shakespeare: From Metaphor to Metamorphosis*. New Haven: Yale University Press, 1974.

Gesner, Carol. *Shakespeare and the Greek Romance*. Lexington: University Press of Kentucky, 1970.

Halio, Jay L. *A Midsummer Night's Dream*. New York: St. Martin's Press, 1994.

Henze, Richard. "*A Midsummer Night's Dream:* Analogous Image." *Shakespeare Studies* 7 (1974): 115–23.

Howard, Skiles. "Hands, Feet, and Bottoms: Decentering the Cosmic Dance in *A Midsummer Night's Dream.*" *Shakespeare Quarterly* 44 (1993): 325–42.

Hunt, Maurice. "The Voices of *A Midsummer Night's Dream.*" *Texas Studies in Literature and Language* 34 (1992): 218–38.

Hunter, Robert G. *Shakespeare and the Comedy of Forgiveness*. New York: Columbia University Press, 1965.

Kott, Jan. *The Bottom Translation*. Tr. Daniela Miedzyrzecka and Lillian Vallee. Evanston, IL: Northwestern University Press, 1987.

Lamb, M. E. "*A Midsummer Night's Dream:* The Myth of Theseus and the Minotaur." *Texas Studies in Literature and Language* 21 (1979): 478–91.

Langley, T. R. "Shakespeare's Dream and Tempest." *Cambridge Quarterly* 20 (1991): 118–37.

Latham, Minor White. *The Elizabethan Fairies: The Fairies of Folklore and the Fairies of Shakespeare*. New York: Columbia University Press, 1930.

Mattis, Olivia. "Theater as Circus: *A Midsummer's Night's Dream.*" *Library Chronicle of the University of Texas* 23, No. 4 (1993): 42–77.

Mebane, John S. "Structure, Source, and Meaning in *A Midsummer Night's Dream.*" *Texas Studies in Literature and Language* 24 (1982): 255–70.

Ormerod, David. "*A Midsummer Night's Dream:* The Monster in the Labyrinth." *Shakespeare Studies* 2 (1978): 39–52.

Patterson, Annabel. "Bottom's Up: Festive Theory." In Patterson's *Shakespeare and the Popular Voice.* Oxford: Basil Blackwell, 1989, pp. 52–70.

Phialas, Peter. *Shakespeare's Romantic Comedies: The Development of Their Form and Meaning.* Chapel Hill: University of North Carolina Press, 1966.

Plasse, Marie A. "The Human Body as Performance Medium in Shakespeare: Some Theatrical Suggestions from *A Midsummer Night's Dream.*" *College Literature* 19 (1992): 28–47.

Rhoads, Diana Akers. *Shakespeare's Defense of Poetry:* A Midsummer Night's Dream *and* The Tempest. Lanham, MD: University Press of America, 1985.

Schanzer, Ernest. "The Central Theme of *A Midsummer Night's Dream.*" *University of Toronto Quarterly* 24 (1951): 233–38.

Schwartz, Robert Barnett. "When Everything Seems Double: *A Midsummer Night's Dream.*" In Schwartz's *Shakespeare's Parted Eye: Perception, Knowledge and Meaning in the Sonnets and Plays.* New York: Peter Lang, 1990, pp. 49–80.

Taylor, Marion A. *Bottom, Thou Art Translated: Political Allegory in* A Midsummer Night's Dream *and Related Literature.* Amsterdam: Rodopi, 1973.

Taylor, Michael. "The Darker Purpose of *A Midsummer Night's Dream.*" *Studies in English Literature* 9 (1969): 259–73.

Weiner, Andrew D. " 'Multiformitie Uniforme': *A Midsummer Night's Dream.*" *ELH* (1971): 329–49.

Wells, Stanley. "*A Midsummer Night's Dream* Revisited." *Critical Survey* 3 (1991): 14–29.

Yachnin, Paul. "The Politics of Theatrical Mirth: *A Midsummer Night's Dream, A Mad World, My Masters,* and *Measure for Measure.*" *Shakespeare Quarterly* 43 (1992): 51–66.

Young, David P. *Something of Great Constancy: The Art of* A Midsummer Night's Dream. New Haven: Yale University Press, 1966.

————. *The Heart's Forest: A Study of Shakespeare's Pastoral Plays.* New Haven: Yale University Press, 1972.

Zimbardo, Rose A. "Regeneration and Reconciliation in *A Midsummer Night's Dream.*" *Shakespeare Studies* 6 (1972): 35–50.

Zitner, Sheldon. P. "The Worlds of *A Midsummer Night's Dream.*" *South Atlantic Quarterly* 59 (1960): 397–403.

Zukovsky, Louis. *Bottom on Shakespeare.* Austin, TX: Ark Press, 1963. 2 vols.

Index of
Themes and Ideas